Self-Sufficiency
Preserving
JAMS, JELLIES, PICKLES AND MORE

Carol Wilson

IMM **lifestyle**
:: books™

Read. Learn. Do What You Love.

Published 2016—IMM Lifestyle Books
www.IMMLifestyleBooks.com

IMM Lifestyle Books are distributed in the UK by Grantham Book Service.

In North America, IMM Lifestyle Books are distributed by
Fox Chapel Publishing
1970 Broad Street
East Petersburg, PA 17520
www.FoxChapelPublishing.com

ISBN 978 1 5048 0035 8

10 9 8 7 6 5 4 3 2 1

Printed in Singapore

The author and publishers have made every effort to ensure that all information
given in this book is safe and accurate, but they cannot accept liability for any
resulting injury or loss or damage to either property or person,
whether direct or consequential or however arising.

CONTENTS

INTRODUCTION

There's something very satisfying about opening a cupboard and surveying the splendid rows of gleaming glass jars filled with homemade jams, jellies, chutneys pickles and bottled fruits. It always gives me a warm glow of achievement to know that all these delicious preserves are homemade from garden produce – if not my own then from a local farmer or smallholder at a farmers' market.

Preserving fruits and vegetables is one of the oldest culinary traditions. Fruit preserves have a long history – the ancient Greeks used to preserve quinces by packing them into jars filled with honey and storing them until the fruit was soft. The arrival of sugar in Europe caused a revolution in the kitchen and by the 17th century it was more readily available and affordable, and preserving fruits with sugar became very fashionable.

Preserving vegetables with salt and/or vinegar has also been practised since ancient times. Pickles were enjoyed in antiquity – Julius Caesar was reputed to have been very fond of pickles and Samuel Pepys mentions enjoying pickled 'girkins' in his famous diary. Pickled gherkins and cucumbers began to be made in the 16th century in Germany and are still enormously popular there and elsewhere, as is sauerkraut (salted fermented cabbage).

All types of preserves were originally made to preserve fruits and vegetables from an all too fleeting summer and autumn, ready for consumption during the cold, harsh winter months. A good harvest of summer and autumn crops could produce an abundance of fruits and vegetables; too many to be eaten immediately and in the days before refrigeration, these needed to be preserved before they perished.

Fermented foods are a rich source of vitamins and minerals, as the process of fermentation increases the amounts of certain vitamins.

Different methods of preserving were created to prevent the food from decaying and to enable its consumption out of season; but gradually as time passed, preserved foods became popular foods in their own right – sweet jams and jellies provided deliciously fruity spreads for plain bread and cakes; bottled fruits kept their shape and colour and could be enjoyed all year round; pickled and salted foods enhanced the taste of bland meals, and all could be enjoyed out of season. We still enjoy preserves today – who can resist a spoonful of homemade fragrant scarlet strawberry jam to brighten up simple bread and butter, or a helping of piquant chutney or pickles to enliven a plate of cheese or cold meats?

Previous generations had to preserve the culinary riches of summer and autumn for the bleak winter months out of necessity. Country housewives collected produce from cottage gardens and from the hedgerows, woods and fields, and preserved them with sugar, salt or vinegar. Some, such as bottled gooseberries and quince paste, were treasured as delicacies and were kept until Christmas to enjoy as a special treat.

The advent of refrigerators and freezers meant that people no longer had to rely on the old methods and the art of preserving was sadly almost lost for a while. Thankfully, self sufficiency is back in vogue, partly from a desire for high quality foods with that inimitable real homemade taste, and partly from a wish to enjoy traditional cooking and preserving. It is important that these skills are not lost, but making your own preserves is not only enjoyable but will save you money, too.

In our great-grandmothers' day it was considered the norm for families to go out to gather fruits and vegetables in season, ready for 'putting up preserves' in marathon cooking sessions. Nowadays, thanks to modern kitchens and equipment, it is quicker and easier than ever to make tasty preserves.

Gardens, allotments, shops and the countryside all provide an abundance of produce in season and conserving a glut of seasonal produce is a time-honoured method of filling the kitchen larder. Whether your produce is home grown from your garden or allotment, gathered from the wild or a farm nearby, or bought from a shop to take advantage of a seasonal glut being sold cheaply, finding a ready supply of produce has never been easier.

Homemade preserves make great presents and are much appreciated by the recipient. They are always popular at food fairs and markets and are a wonderful way of raising funds for charity fundraisers. I've always enjoyed making preserves for friends and family, who love to receive them as gifts. There's a particular pleasure in giving something you've made yourself and of course they taste so much better than large-scale commercial versions, which are often horribly oversweet or crammed with additives. What could be better than a shimmering amethyst blackberry jam or jelly made from freshly picked sun-ripened berries, or tangy pickled crunchy vegetables?

The preserving methods in this book are clearly explained, together with details of the equipment needed, information on ingredients, cooking techniques and storage instructions. The tried-and-tested recipes are clear and easy to follow with step-by-step instructions, plus a section at the end of each chapter on what can go wrong – usually this happens if a recipe isn't followed correctly or the preserves are incorrectly stored.

You'll find some old favourites as well as new and unusual preserves that will please you, your family and friends – and of course they have the added appeal of being made with love and care.

PRESERVING

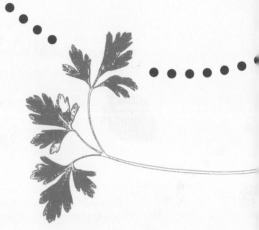

There are several different methods of preserving fruits and vegetables and all give delicious results. Jams, jellies, fruit butters and curds, bottled fruits, chutneys, pickles and salted vegetables are all practical and economical ways to preserve seasonal produce.

Types of preserve

Jam is a thick mixture of fruit and sugar, cooked until the pieces of fruit are very soft and almost formless. Fruit jams were originally regarded as luxury foods and saved for celebrations and holidays.

Jelly is a crystal clear, translucent mixture made from fruit juice, sugar and sometimes pectin. It should be brilliantly clear and the texture should wobble, but still hold its shape.

Marmalade was originally a medieval confection made from quinces. Marmalades made from other fruits such as cherries and plums appeared in the 17th century, although these marmalades would not be familiar to us today, as they were firm enough to slice and were eaten as a dessert. As time passed, only citrus fruits were used to make marmalade. The first orange marmalade was made from bitter Seville oranges.

Fruit butter and curd don't necessarily contain butter; the name refers to their velvety, almost creamy texture, which is stiffer and smoother than that of jam. Fruit butters are soft and spreadable, while curds are thicker. Both have only a short shelf life as they don't contain

"all these methods are both practical and economical ways of preserving seasonal produce"

as much sugar in proportion to fruit as jam, so are usually made in small quantities and stored in the refrigerator.

Chutney is a sweet-spicy relish made with sugar and vinegar. It originated in India (the name comes from *chatni*, meaning a strong, sweet relish) and first appeared in Europe in the 17th century, when it became very popular for pepping up bland foods. Chutney is cooked slowly to produce a rich, full flavour and may be very hot and spicy or mild and aromatic, depending on the ingredients used.

Pickles are a time-honoured method of preserving vegetables in a brine or vinegar mixture and may be sour, sweet, hot or mild. The English word 'pickle' is derived from the medieval word *pikel*, which meant 'a spicy sauce served with meat or fowl', which is related to the Middle Dutch word *pekel*, meaning a solution (usually spiced brine) for preserving and flavouring food. Vinegar is a powerful preservative as few bacteria can survive in its acidic environment. The vegetables stay crisp and develop a tangy flavour. Cucumbers are the most commonly pickled vegetables in Eastern Europe, often with spices, herbs, and sometimes a few oak or cherry leaves are added to the vinegar for extra flavour.

Bottling fruit is a practice that dates back to antiquity; the ancient Romans filled jars with fruits and covered them with juice, wine, vinegar or honey, then sealed the jars to make them airtight. Nowadays bottled fruits are prepared by sterilising the fruit in large wide-necked jars, so that the fruit stays whole. Any fruit can be bottled, including fruits such as peaches and tomatoes, which can't be preserved by freezing. Bottled fruit keeps indefinitely and is ready to serve as soon as it is made. As the fruit remains whole, bottled fruit is usually eaten as a dessert with cream, ice cream or custard, or used in trifle, etc.

Salting vegetables is an ancient method of preservation and is excellent for preserving runner and French beans in particular, which have a completely different flavour from canned or frozen beans. In Eastern Europe salting vegetables and even some fruits is a common practice. Salted white cabbage (sauerkraut) is left until it has fermented and is particularly popular in Germany and Eastern Europe. Fermented foods are a rich source of vitamins and minerals, as the process of fermentation increases the amounts of certain vitamins; sauerkraut for instance is a very good source of vitamin C and was often included in military rations in ancient armies and was used to prevent scurvy.

Jams, jellies and marmalades

These jewel-coloured fruit preserves have been popular for hundreds of years and are an economical way of using up a glut of fruit and wonderful for preserving the flavours of luscious seasonal fruits to enjoy all year round. They are delicious as a spread for bread, a filling for tarts and sponge cakes and melted as a dessert sauce for ice cream.

Equipment

Use a large, deep heavy-based pan with plenty of room for the mixture to boil rapidly without boiling over. Special preserving pans are available, which are wider at the top with sloping sides to aid evaporation and ensure setting point is reached more quickly. It's worth investing in a preserving pan if you intend to make a tlot of preserves.

A sturdy wooden spoon with a long handle is best to ensure your hands are not too close to the boiling mixture when stirring.

A sugar/preserving thermometer is useful, but not essential, to test that the correct temperature for setting point has been reached.

For jelly-making you will need a jelly bag (from cookware shops) which should be scalded first by pouring boiling water through it, so that the fruit juices don't soak into it.

A wide funnel is helpful when filling the jars, but a jug or a small ladle can be used instead.

Kilner (Mason) jars are ideal for storing homemade preserves and come in a range of sizes. A Kilner jar is a glass jar which has a lid in two sections to ensure an airtight seal. Originally a glass disc sat on top of the jar and was then secured in place with a metal screw band containing a rubber seal. Nowadays both sections of the lid are usually made from metal. The original Kilner jar is sometimes mistaken for the more widely available glass jar with a rubber seal and a metal

hinge, which when closed forms an
airtight seal. These jars can be used
instead of Kilner jars.

You can buy special packs
containing glass jars and
lids and also packs of
waxed circles (these are placed
waxed-side down on top of the
potted preserve, while still hot, to
exclude air and prevent deterioration),
transparent cellophane covers (dampened
and placed on top of the potted preserve when
it is completely cold, then secured with an elastic
band. The cellophane shrinks as it dries to form a tight
seal over the jar), and elastic bands in varying sizes from cookware and
kitchen shops. Don't use the same equipment for vinegar preserves when
making jam as cross contamination will spoil the flavour of the jam.

Sterilising jars
Jars must be scrupulously clean and warm before being filled to
the brim to allow for shrinkage. Wash the jars in hot soapy water,
rinse very well and put in a low oven for 15–20 minutes until
warm and completely dry. Sterilise the lids in boiling water for
10 minutes, keeping them in the hot water until ready for use,
then dry thoroughly with kitchen paper (paper towels). An old
country method to discourage mould forming in stored jams was
to brush the surface of the jar lids or the waxed discs with brandy
before placing them over the hot jam.

Ingredients

Fruit for jams and jellies must be completely dry, firm, fresh and ripe or slightly underripe, but don't use overripe produce, as this may cause the finished preserve to ferment during storage. There's no need to remove stones that are difficult to dislodge from fruit – when the jam is boiling the stones will float to the top and can be taken out then.

Fruit is prepared according to type when making jam, but there's no need to do this when making jelly as the fruit is strained in a jelly bag and the pips, cores, skins, etc., are left in the jelly bag during the straining process.

Popular fruits for jams and jellies

Apples come in all shades of reds, greens and yellows and may be sweet, tart, soft and smooth or crisp and crunchy, depending on the variety. Cooking apples are larger and have a sharper flavour than eating apples.

Apricots have fragrant juicy flesh with a large kernel in the centre that can be removed easily if the fruit is ripe.

Blackberries are best when plump and ripe and full of juice. Cultivated blackberries lack the deep flavour of wild berries but are still delicious and have the advantage of having fewer pips than the wild variety.

Blackcurrants have a rich, strong, sharp flavour and the dark purple berries are very popular for making into jam.

Blueberries, also known as whortleberries or huckleberries have a slight dusty bloom and tart flavour. They should be ripe but firm.

Cherries may be almost black, bright red, pale pink or yellow in colour. It's best to taste them before buying to check if they're sweet enough for your taste.

Elderberries are the purple-black fruit of the elder tree. They must never be eaten raw and are always cooked.

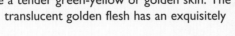

Gooseberries may be green, yellow or red, although the sour green berries are the best for cooking.

Mulberries are similar to black-berries but are more elongated and may be white, red or black. They have a mild sweet flavour and make excellent jams.

Peaches, when ripe, have a fragrant odour and the velvety skin may be red, blushed pink or yellow, or white. One side of the fruit has a distinctive vertical indentation.

Pears have fine, soft, juicy flesh which, unusually, improves in both flavour and texture after they're picked. The skin may be bronze, green, pink or red.

Plums may be blue, green, purple, red or yellow. The flesh is thick and juicy and the flavour ranges from sweet to tart. Damsons are a variety of plum, much smaller than cultivated plums, with a tart, strong flavour. When cooked their flavour has a faint hint of almonds with a touch of spice. Damsons are indigestible when raw, but the sharp tasting fruit is transformed during cooking and makes wonderful preserves. Greengages have a tender green-yellow or golden skin. The translucent golden flesh has an exquisitely

"preserving sugar dissolves quicker and creates less foam than ordinary sugar"

sweet flavour and it is regarded as one of the finest dessert plums. Victoria plums have yellow- to rose-coloured skins and their pink-hued flesh is rich, sweet and juicy when ripe. Before the fruit is fully ripe it is particularly good for making preserves.

Quinces are exquisitely perfumed and although hard and inedible when raw, make delectable preserves. The fruit has a yellowish-green skin covered with down which is scrubbed off before using.

Raspberries are sweet and fragrant with a velvety texture. Choose bright firm berries, which may be red or yellow.

Rhubarb is actually a vegetable but is often eaten as a fruit. 'Forced' rhubarb should have tender pink stems, which have a refreshingly tart flavour. There's no need to peel young rhubarb, just remove any stringy bits. When using outdoor grown rhubarb choose red stems – if the stems are green the flavour will be very sour and acid. It is important to note that rhubarb leaves are highly poisonous and must be discarded.

Strawberries have a glorious scented flavour and soft luscious texture. Choose firm, plump, scarlet berries with very few green or white patches. Very large berries often lack flavour. Don't wash them until just before you want to use them.

Rinse the fruits very gently and hull the berries *after* washing to avoid making them soggy – the hull acts as a 'plug'.

Sugar is the preserving agent and granulated white sugar is fine. It is not essential to buy special preserving sugar, although the larger crystals dissolve quickly and create less foam than ordinary sugar and produce a clearer, more translucent jam. Preserving sugar is meant to be used with fruits high in pectin, such as gooseberries and blackcurrants. Jam sugar is granulated sugar with added pectin and is designed for fruits low in pectin, such as strawberries, cherries and rhubarb. Caster or brown sugar is not recommended (unless specifically stated in the ingredients) as these tend to produce a lot of foam.

Pectin, a natural gelling agent found in ripe fruit, helps jam and jelly to set. The amount of pectin present depends on the type of fruit and its ripeness. Some fruits, including apples, blackcurrants and quinces have high levels of pectin, while others such as cherries, elderberries and strawberries are low in pectin and must have additional pectin added for good results. Lemon juice, which is naturally high in pectin, or commercial liquid or powdered pectin should be added in this case, and this will be stated in the recipe.

Other types of sugar

Demerara: large, sparkling golden crystals with a sticky, crunchy texture and light molasses flavour.
Light muscovado: moist, fine-grained crystals with a rich aroma and glorious fudgy flavour.
Dark muscovado: a dark brown sugar with a sticky texture and rich toffee flavour.
Molasses: the richest of all the sugars, with a distinctive deep, dark, treacly flavour.

Cooking

Jams

Warm the sugar first by spreading it on a baking tray and placing in a low oven at 120°C/250°F (gas ½) for about 10 minutes before adding to the fruit and water to enable it to dissolve more quickly.

Lightly greasing the inside of the pan with butter before you start making jam will help to reduce the amount of foam on the surface of the boiling mixture. The pan should never be more than half full to ensure sufficient space for rapid boiling after the sugar has been added. The fruit should simmer slowly at first to ensure that all the pectin is extracted. Cover the pan while the fruit is simmering.

The sugar is added when the fruit is soft and should be allowed to dissolve completely before the mixture is brought to the boil. Whichever type of sugar you use, it must be completely dissolved before the mixture is brought to the boil. If the sugar is not dissolved completely when the mixture starts boiling, the preserve will be difficult to set and is likely to crystallise during storage. To test if the sugar is dissolved, dip a wooden spoon in the mixture, and if no sugar crystals are visible in the liquid that coats the back of the spoon, it will have dissolved. Uncover the pan when the sugar has been added and stir only occasionally to prevent sticking and burning.

"the pan should never be more than half full to ensure sufficient space for rapid boiling"

As it cools, the jam will begin to set and will wrinkle when pushed gently with your finger and will remain in two separate parts when you draw your finger through it.

The mixture should then boil steadily and rapidly to ensure setting point is reached in the shortest time. Don't stir the mixture continually while it is boiling as this will lower the temperature and delay the setting point.

A good set depends on the amounts of pectin, acid (naturally found in fruit) and sugar. Acid helps to release the pectin which works with sugar to form a gel and set the jam. Some jams will reach setting point after just a few minutes' boiling, while others will take 15 minutes or more.

To tell when setting point has been reached, remove the pan from the heat and put a teaspoon of the boiling mixture on a chilled saucer. As it cools, the jam will begin to set and will wrinkle when pushed gently with your finger and will remain in two separate parts when you draw your finger through it. It is a good idea to have ready three or four saucers in the freezer or refrigerator for testing purposes.

If using a sugar thermometer, keep this in warm water until ready to use, so that the temperature of the boiling jam isn't reduced too much when you put it into the mixture.

Don't let the thermometer touch the base of
the pan or you may get a false reading. Turn the
thermometer around in the mixture, so that you have
an accurate reading. It should read 104°C (220°F).

If setting point hasn't been reached, return to the heat and
boil for a few minutes only before testing again. Don't overcook;
if the mixture is boiled for too long it won't set.

If using whole fruits, the recipe will state to let the hot jam stand for
several minutes before pouring into jars. This is so that the fruit does not
rise to the top of the jars when the jam is potted. If the jam or jars are
too hot, fruit will rise to the top, spoiling the appearance of the finished
product. When setting point has been reached, remove the pan from
the heat and let the mixture stand for about 10–15 minutes, until
a skin forms on the surface. Skim off any foam and stir once
to distribute the fruit, before pouring into the warmed jars.
Alternatively, after removing the pan from the heat, stir in a
small knob of butter to disperse the foam.

Stand the warmed jars on folded newspaper or
a wooden board to prevent cracking when the hot
jam or jelly is poured in. Pour the mixture into the jars,
filling them to the brim, as the jam will shrink a little as it
cools. The less air space there is in the jars, the better the
jam or jelly will keep.

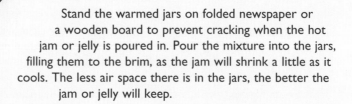

Store in a cool, dark, dry and ventilated place as preserves tend to lose a little colour if exposed to light.

Wipe the outside of the filled jars and cover
the surface of the hot jam with waxed
circles, waxed side down. If you forget to
cover the jam with the discs while the
jam is still hot, leave until completely
cold, otherwise mould
may grow on the surface if the jam
is covered while only warm.

Now allow the jam to cool before applying
the wetted cellophane covers. If these are
applied before the jam is cooled, water can
condense inside the covers, causing mould.

Seal tightly with either plastic lids, metal screw top lids or wetted
cellophane covers (wetted side up) and elastic bands. Transparent
cellophane covers will shrink as they dry to form a tight seal.

Finally, label with the name of the jam and the date, and store in a cool,
dark, dry and well ventilated place. Some preserves tend to lose a little
colour if exposed to light. A warm, moist atmosphere will cause the jam
to shrink, and dampness will encourage mould. Most jams will keep
for up to a year. Once opened store in the refrigerator.

Jellies

Making jelly is almost identical to making jam and the equipment is much the same. However, you will also need a jelly bag. This is made of heavy-duty cotton, muslin or nylon with a very close weave. The bag must be scalded with boiling water before use to sterilise it and to avoid the fruit juices soaking into the bag.

Fruits high in pectin, such as blackcurrants, redcurrants and gooseberries are best for jelly making. Those with a low pectin content, such as blackberries or cherries are best combined with a high-pectin fruit, such as redcurrants or apples, or made using sugar with pectin. There's no need to stone, hull or core fruit for jellies as the cooked mixture is strained through a jelly bag. The fruit should be cooked slowly to extract the pectin.

Suspend the jelly bag from a hook or from the legs of an upturned stool or chair and place a large bowl underneath to catch the juice. Ladle the fruit pulp and juices into the jelly bag and leave to drip into the bowl for several hours or overnight. Don't squeeze the bag to speed up the process or the jelly will be cloudy.

"fruits high in pectin – blackcurrants, redcurrants and gooseberries – are best for jelly making"

The juice is then boiled with the sugar until setting point is reached – the amount of sugar needed depends on the type and weight of the fruits used and will be stated in the recipe. The cooking time can vary from 30 minutes to over 1 hour, according to the ripeness of the fruit. Because of the method used to extract the juice, it is difficult to estimate the final amount produced, so it is best to have ready more warmed jars than you think you will need. As a general guide, 1 kg (2 lb) sugar should make about 1.5 kg (3 lb) jelly. Jellies are best potted as soon as possible; if left to stand they start to gel in the pan.

The high temperature causes the pectin to react, so the boiling mixture must not be stirred, although you can skim off the foam that rises to the top as the mixture boils.

Jelly is potted in the same way as jam (see page 23). Remove any foam from the top of the jelly with a metal spoon or stir slowly to disperse. To avoid air bubbles forming, tilt the jar and pour in the hot jelly slowly. Seal and label. Don't move the jars until the jelly has set completely. Once opened store in the refrigerator.

Marmalade

Marmalade is made in the same way as jam (see page 23), but because it is made with citrus fruit it needs a longer cooking time. The tough peel needs to be cooked for longer until soft, so more water is required. The same equipment is required for making marmalade as for jams and jellies, with the addition of a sharp knife and a juice extractor.

Bitter or Seville oranges, with their fragrant aromatic peel and intensely flavoured astringent juice, are frequently used in marmalades. Use a zester or potato peeler to remove the rind. Don't include the white pith as this will give a bitter taste.

Lemons have a sharp citrus flavour. Choose thin-skinned fruits (those with thicker peel will have less flesh and therefore be less juicy) that are heavy for their size and bright yellow. Avoid any that are tinged with green as they're not fully ripe and will be very acidic. Use unwaxed citrus fruits if possible; otherwise the fruit must be well scrubbed under hot running water, to remove the protective waxy coating of fungicide. Use a potato peeler to remove the rind in thin strips and don't include the white pith.

Don't include the white pith in your marmalade, as this will give a bitter taste.

Limes are oval or round in shape with green flesh and skin and are more fragrant than lemons. Choose limes that are firm and heavy for their size, with deep green shiny skin. Use unwaxed fruits if possible.

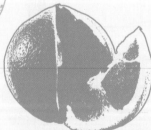

Grapefruit are large citrus fruits with a refreshingly tart

flavour and yellow or pink rind and are available in both seeded and seedless varieties. Choose fruits that are heavy for their size (which indicates a good amount of juicy flesh) and a sweet aroma.

Citrus fruits must be well scrubbed to remove any waxy coating or fungicide and then dried thoroughly. The peel may be cut finely or coarsely, according to preference. The pectin, which gives the set, is mainly contained in the pith and pips, so these must not be discarded but tied loosely in a piece of muslin and added to the pan. The secret of good marmalade is fast boiling: test after 15 minutes, then every 5 minutes after that. Test for setting in the same way as for jam (see page 22–3).

When setting point has been reached, remove the pan from the heat and let the mixture stand for about 10–20 minutes, when a skin will form on the surface. This prevents the peel rising to the surface after potting. Stir once before pouring into the jars so the peel will be suspended evenly in the jelly.

Cover the marmalade with a waxed disc when hot, but seal with a cellophane cover or lid when cold to prevent condensation.

What can go wrong?

Mouldy or fermented jam, jelly or marmalade occurs if the preserve is potted while warm (instead of hot or cold), if the jars are unsterilised, insufficiently covered or sealed, or if stored in a damp place. If there is just a thin layer of greyish-white mould on top of the jam or jelly, scrape it off completely and taste the preserve. If it tastes pleasant, then it can be eaten and should be stored in the refrigerator. If the mould is evident throughout the preserve, then it will be inedible and should be thrown away.

Crystallisation (small sugary crystals that form during storage) occurs if the sugar is not completely dissolved before boiling, if too much sugar is used for the proportion of fruit or if the preserve is cooked for too long. As this can't be rectified it is probably best to use the jam or jelly as a hot sauce.

Dull jam, jelly or marmalade is due to cooking too long after adding the sugar.

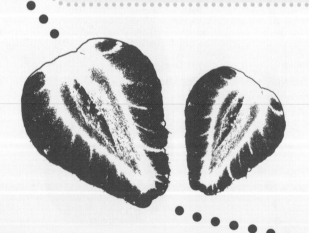

"dull jam, jelly or marmalade is due to cooking too long after adding the sugar"

Bubbles dispersed in jelly is due to leaving the jelly too long before potting, causing it to over-thicken, trapping bubbles of air. Foam that hasn't been removed before potting will also spoil the appearance of a jelly but won't affect the taste.

Cloudy jelly is due to pressing or squeezing the jelly bag in an attempt to speed up the process while the juice is dripping through the bag.

Fruit pieces rising in the jam are due to potting it too soon. The jam should be allowed to rest for the time stated in the recipe before transferring into jars.

Tough marmalade peel is due to the peel not being sufficiently softened in the fruit juice before adding the sugar. This cannot be remedied once the marmalade is made so check that the peel is very soft before adding the sugar.

Very dark, sticky jam or marmalade means it was overcooked.

Stiff and rubbery jam is caused by using wrong proportions, usually insufficient sugar and water for the quantity of fruit.

Jam shrinking away from the sides of the jar is caused by boiling for too long or not creating an airtight seal when covering the jars. Re-cover the jars to prevent further evaporation.

Runny jam or jelly is caused by using overripe fruit or insufficient pectin, too much sugar or not boiling for long enough. Use it as a sauce instead.

"If your jam or jelly is too runny use it as a sauce rather than wasting it"

Apple and blackberry jam

This combination of fruits is an old country favourite. Blackberries are low in pectin but because the apples have a high pectin level this jam sets well. In late summer and early autumn blackberries grow profusely in the wild and these have more flavour than the cultivated variety.

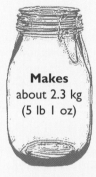

Makes
about 2.3 kg
(5 lb 1 oz)

☑ 675 g (1 lb 8 oz) cooking apples, peeled and cored weight

☑ 150 ml (5 fl oz) water

☑ 1 kg (2 lb 3 oz) blackberries

☑ 1.4 kg (3 lb 2 oz) granulated or caster sugar

1 Chop the apples into small pieces and put into a large heavy-based pan with the water. Bring to the boil, then simmer gently for 10 minutes.

2 Add the blackberries and continue to simmer gently for another 10 minutes, until the mixture is a soft purée.

3 Stir in the sugar until completely dissolved, then bring back to the boil. Boil rapidly for about 15–20 minutes, until setting point is reached.

4 Remove the pan from the heat. Pour into warmed sterilised jars, then cover, seal and label.

Apple, pear and plum jam

This was a popular 19th century recipe and is a delicious way to use up a glut of seasonal fruit, and windfall apples and pears. You can use any variety of fruit in this recipe. Plums come in dozens of varieties, shapes, sizes and colours, ranging from green to red, through deep purple to almost black.

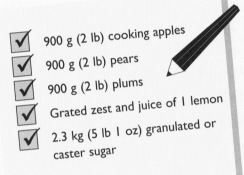

☑ 900 g (2 lb) cooking apples

☑ 900 g (2 lb) pears

☑ 900 g (2 lb) plums

☑ Grated zest and juice of 1 lemon

☑ 2.3 kg (5 lb 1 oz) granulated or caster sugar

1 Peel and core the apples and pears. Cut the plums in half and remove the stones. Put all the fruit into a large heavy-based pan with the lemon zest and juice.

2 Heat gently to boiling point, then reduce the heat, cover the pan and simmer very gently until the fruit is soft – if it starts to stick to the pan add a little water. The actual cooking time needed will depend on the ripeness of the fruit.

3 Stir in the sugar until completely dissolved, then bring to the boil. Boil rapidly for about 15–20 minutes, until setting point is reached.

4 Remove the pan from the heat. Pour into warmed sterilised jars, then cover, seal and label.

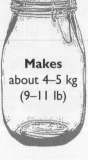

Makes
about 4–5 kg
(9–11 lb)

Apricot jam

Beautiful orange apricots are one of the first fruits of summer. The fruit is low in pectin so lemon juice is added to the recipe. You could also use sugar that contains pectin. Add the kernels to the jam just before setting point is reached, otherwise they will become too soft.

Makes
about 3 kg
(6 lb 10 oz)

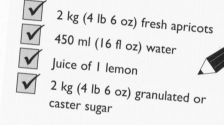

☑ 2 kg (4 lb 6 oz) fresh apricots
☑ 450 ml (16 fl oz) water
☑ Juice of 1 lemon
☑ 2 kg (4 lb 6 oz) granulated or caster sugar

1 Cut the apricots in half and remove the stones. Crack 6–8 stones to remove the kernels and blanch the kernels by dipping them in boiling water for 1 minute. These will give extra flavour to the jam.

2 Put the fruit into a large heavy-based pan with the water and bring to the boil. Reduce the heat and simmer gently for about 20 minutes until soft.

3 Stir in the lemon juice and sugar until completely dissolved, then bring to the boil. Boil rapidly for about 15–20 minutes, until setting point is reached. Add the kernels to the pan just before setting point is reached.

4 Remove the pan from the heat. Pour into warmed sterilised jars, then cover, seal and label.

Bilberry (blueberry) jam

The small dark purple berries have a faint dusty 'bloom' and are also known as blueberries or whortlebeberries. The berries grow on bushes and have a distinctive, richly aromatic but tart flavour. The skins soften quickly and their pectin content ensures the jam sets quickly.

☑ 450 g (1 lb) bilberries
☑ 450 g (1 lb) granulated or caster sugar

Makes
about 675 g
(1 lb 8 oz)

1 Put the bilberries into a large heavy-based pan. Heat gently to boiling point, then reduce the heat, cover the pan and simmer very gently for about 10 minutes until the fruit is soft and the juices begin to flow. The actual time will depend on the ripeness of the fruit.

2 Stir in the sugar until completely dissolved, then bring to the boil. Boil rapidly for about 10–15 minutes, until setting point is reached.

3 Remove the pan from the heat. Pour into warmed sterilised jars, then cover, seal and label.

Blackcurrant jam

These astringent little blueish-black berries grow on shrubs and have a sweet-sharp flavour. They have high levels of health-boosting antioxidants – natural compounds (responsible for the fruit's dark colour) which are credited with the ability to stave off a range of illnesses.

1 Strip the berries from the stalks with a fork into a large heavy-based pan. Add the water and slowly bring to the boil. Reduce the heat and simmer gently for about 20–30 minutes until the fruit is soft.

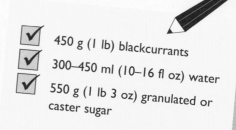

✓ 450 g (1 lb) blackcurrants
✓ 300–450 ml (10–16 fl oz) water
✓ 550 g (1 lb 3 oz) granulated or caster sugar

2 Add the sugar and stir over a low heat until the sugar has dissolved completely. Bring to the boil and boil rapidly for about 10–15 minutes, until setting point is reached.

3 Remove the pan from the heat. Pour into warmed sterilised jars, then cover, seal and label.

Makes
about 1 kg
(2 lb 3 oz)

Cherry jam

Cherries can be very dark, almost black, bright red, pale pink or yellow.
Small, dark red, wild cherries are also known as 'geans' (from the French guine)
and may be sweet or bitter. Leaving the cherry stones in while you cook them
imparts a delicate almond flavour to the finished jam.

 675 g (1 lb 8 oz) firm dessert cherries

 2 Tbsp water

 1 Tbsp lemon juice

 400 g (14 oz) granulated or caster sugar

1 Put the cherries into a large heavy-based pan with the water. The stones add flavour to the jam and can be removed when the jam is boiling.

2 Heat gently to boiling point, then reduce the heat, cover the pan and simmer very gently until the fruit is soft – if it starts to stick to the pan add a little more water. The actual time will depend on the ripeness of the fruit.

3 Stir in the lemon juice and sugar until completely dissolved, then bring to the boil. Boil rapidly for about 15–20 minutes, until setting point is reached.

4 Remove the pan from the heat, then remove the stones with a slotted spoon. Allow to stand for a few minutes and stir to distribute the fruit. Pour into warmed sterilised jars, then cover, seal and label.

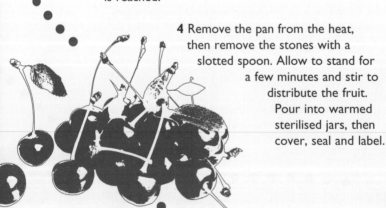

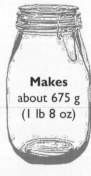

Makes
about 675 g
(1 lb 8 oz)

Gooseberry and elderflower jam

Although red and yellow varieties of gooseberry are sweeter than green, the small, hard, green berries are best for cooking as they have more flavour. The raw berries are sharp and sour tasting, but their acidity is transformed when cooking them with sugar. Elderflowers add a delicate muscat flavour. Pick the creamy white flowers well away from the roadside and traffic fumes, give them a gentle shake to dislodge any insects and rinse briefly in cold water before using.

1 Put the gooseberries, elder-flowers and water into a large heavy-based pan.

2 Heat gently to boiling point, then reduce the heat. Cover the pan and simmer very gently for about 20–30 minutes, until the skins are soft, stirring from time to time to prevent the fruit sticking. The actual time will depend on the ripeness of the fruit.

 1.5 kg (3 lb 5 oz) hard, slightly under ripe gooseberries, topped and tailed

 2 small heads of elderflowers, stems removed and tied in muslin

 600 ml (1 pt) water

 1.5 kg (3 lb 5 oz) granulated or caster sugar

3 Stir in the sugar until completely dissolved, then bring to the boil. Boil rapidly for about 15–20 minutes, until setting point is reached.

4 Remove the pan from the heat, then discard the elderflowers. Pour into warmed sterilised jars, then cover, seal and label.

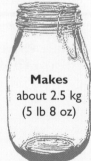

Makes
about 2.5 kg
(5 lb 8 oz)

Greengage jam

Greengages are small- to medium-sized plums with a tender green-yellow or golden skin. The translucent golden flesh is wonderfully sweet. The fruit is high in pectin and produces superb jam.

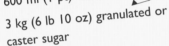

- ✓ 3 kg (6 lb 10 oz) greengages
- ✓ 600 ml (1 pt) water
- ✓ 3 kg (6 lb 10 oz) granulated or caster sugar

1 Cut the fruit in half and remove the stones. If the fruit is too firm to remove the stones easily, cook the fruit with the stones in and remove with a slotted spoon when the jam is boiling.

2 Crack 8–10 stones to remove the kernels and blanch the kernels by dipping them in boiling water for 1 minute. These will give extra flavour to the jam.

3 Put the fruit into a large heavy-based pan with the water and bring to the boil. Reduce the heat and simmer gently for about 30 minutes, until soft. The actual time will depend on the ripeness of the fruit.

4 Stir in the sugar until completely dissolved, then bring to the boil. Boil rapidly for about 15–20 minutes, until setting point is reached. Add the kernels to the pan just before setting point is reached.

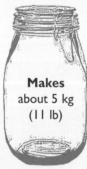

Makes
about 5 kg
(11 lb)

5 Remove the pan from the heat. Pour into warmed sterilised jars, then cover, seal and label.

Marrow and ginger jam

The marrow is a member of the squash family and as it grows it swells up with water, so the flesh is watery with a very delicate, almost insipid flavour. Marrows have long been used to make jam, and ginger is usually included to add a kick to the rather bland taste.

1 Cut the marrow into small pieces. Put into a large heavy-based pan with the sugar and ginger, cover and leave overnight.

☑ 2 kg (4 lb 6 oz) marrow, peeled and seeded weight

☑ 2 kg (4 lb 6 oz) granulated or caster sugar

☑ 6 Tbsp crystallised ginger, finely chopped

☑ Juice of 3 lemons

2 Stir well and place over a low heat, stirring until the sugar has dissolved completely. Add the lemon juice and bring to the boil. Boil steadily for about 30 minutes, until setting point is reached.

3 Remove the pan from the heat. Allow to stand for a few minutes and stir to distribute the marrow pieces. Pour into warmed sterilised jars, then cover, seal and label.

Makes about 3 kg (6 lb 10 oz)

Mulberry and plum jam

Dark crimson mulberries make a luxurious and unusual jam. The medium to large fruit has a yellow to rose coloured skin and the pinkish flesh is rich, sweet and juicy when ripe. Before the fruit is fully ripe it is particularly good for making excellent jam. If you can't get hold of mulberries use blackberries instead.

 1 kg (2 lb 3 oz) mulberries

 1 kg (2 lb 3 oz) Victoria plums

 300 ml (11 fl oz) water

 Granulated or caster sugar

 Juice of 1 lemon

Knob of unsalted butter

1 Put the mulberries and plums in a large heavy-based pan with the water and bring to the boil. Reduce the heat and simmer gently until soft.

2 Press the mixture though a sieve into a bowl. In a measuring jug, measure the mixture back into the pan. To each 600 ml (1 pt) fruit mixture add 450 g (11 lb) sugar.

3 Add the lemon juice and bring slowly to the boil, then boil rapidly for about 15–20 minutes, until setting point is reached.

4 Remove the pan from the heat and stir in the butter. Allow to stand for 5 minutes. Pour into warmed sterilised jars, then cover, seal and label.

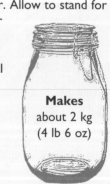

Makes
about 2 kg
(4 lb 6 oz)

Peach and walnut jam

Velvet-skinned, fresh, juicy peaches and crisp-textured walnuts are combined to make an unusual jam with a delightful flavour. Old gardens yield rich tasting walnuts with crinkled surfaces. When young they have a fresh milky flavour and better texture than the rather woody specimens on offer in some shops.

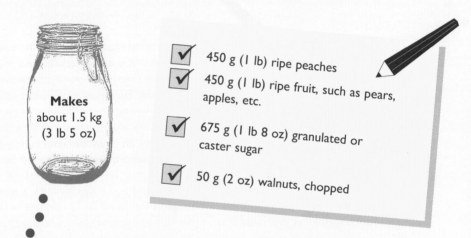

Makes
about 1.5 kg
(3 lb 5 oz)

☑ 450 g (1 lb) ripe peaches

☑ 450 g (1 lb) ripe fruit, such as pears, apples, etc.

☑ 675 g (1 lb 8 oz) granulated or caster sugar

☑ 50 g (2 oz) walnuts, chopped

1 Peel all the fruit and cut into small pieces. Put into a large heavy-based pan with the sugar. Stir over a low heat until completely dissolved, then bring to the boil. Boil rapidly for about 15–20 minutes, until thick and setting point is reached. Stir in the walnuts and boil for 1 minute.

2 Remove the pan from the heat. Pour into warmed sterilised jars, then cover, seal and label.

Raspberry jam

Velvety red or yellow raspberries are among summer's most delicious fruits. Make the most of their fleeting appearance with this beautiful scarlet coloured jam. When sugar became affordable to all in the 18th century it became very fashionable to make jams and preserves from these berries.

☑ 2 kg (4 lb 6 oz) raspberries

☑ 2 kg (4 lb 6 oz) granulated or caster sugar

1 Put the raspberries into a large heavy-based pan. Crush the fruit with a wooden spoon to release the juices. Heat gently to boiling point, then simmer until the juices run.

2 Stir in the sugar until completely dissolved, then bring to the boil.

3 If you prefer a seedless jam, press the fruit and juices through a sieve and return to the rinsed pan. Boil rapidly for about 8–12 minutes until setting point is reached.

4 Remove the pan from the heat. Pour into warmed sterilised jars, then cover, seal and label.

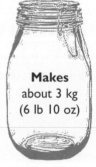

Makes
about 3 kg
(6 lb 10 oz)

Rhubarb and ginger jam

The sharp, fresh taste of rhubarb has a special affinity with ginger. Limp rhubarb can be perked up by standing the stems upright in iced water for about an hour.

Makes
about 2.5 kg
(5 lb 8 oz)

✓ 1.5 kg (3 lb 5 oz) rhubarb, chopped into small pieces

✓ Juice of 1 lemon

✓ 1.3 kg (2 lb 14 oz) granulated or caster sugar

✓ 110 g (4 oz) crystallised ginger, chopped

1 Put the rhubarb, lemon juice and sugar into a large bowl. Cover and leave to stand for 24 hours.

2 Tip the mixture into a large pan and add the ginger. Heat very gently over a low heat until the sugar has dissolved completely, then increase the heat and bring to the boil. Boil rapidly for about 20 minutes until setting point is reached.

3 Remove the pan from the heat. Pour into warmed sterilised jars, then cover, seal and label.

NB: Rhubarb leaves contain oxalic acid, so are highly poisonous and must be discarded.

Strawberry jam

Strawberries are plentiful in the summer and their sunny-scented, fruity flavour makes for superb jam. Rinse the fruits very gently and hull the berries after washing to avoid making them soggy as the hull acts as a 'plug'.

 2 kg (4 lb 6 oz) strawberries

 1.6 kg (3 lb 8 oz) granulated or caster sugar

Juice of 2 large lemons (about 8 Tbsp)

1 Cut any very large strawberries into smaller pieces to speed up the cooking time. Put the strawberries into a large heavy-based pan over a low heat and slowly bring to the boil. Reduce the heat and simmer gently for about 10–15 minutes, until the fruit is softened.

2 Add the sugar and lemon juice and stir over a low heat until the sugar has dissolved completely. Bring to the boil and boil rapidly for about 15–20 minutes, until setting point is reached.

3 Remove the pan from the heat. Skim off any foam and allow the jam to cool for 15 minutes, to ensure the strawberries are distributed evenly. Pour into warmed sterilised jars, then cover, seal and label.

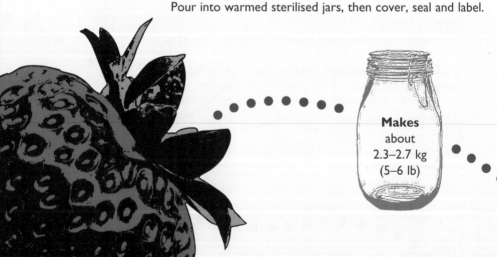

Makes
about
2.3–2.7 kg
(5–6 lb)

Tomato apple jam

Botanically, the tomato is really a fruit and many people used to eat them as a fruit in the past. Tomato jams were popular at the end of the 19th century, when the tomatoes were often combined with other fruit. This sweet preserve is delicious as an accompaniment to cakes or scones and as a topping for steamed pudding.

Makes
about 1.5 kg
(3 lb 5 oz)

 450 g (1 lb) cooking apples, peeled and cored weight

 450 g (1 lb) red tomatoes, skinned and finely chopped

 3 Tbsp water

 1 kg (2 lb 3 oz) granulated or caster sugar

1 Chop the apples finely and put into a large heavy-based pan with the tomatoes and water. Bring to the boil, then simmer gently for about 15 minutes, until the fruits are soft and mushy.

2 Stir in the sugar until completely dissolved, then bring to the boil. Boil rapidly for about 15–20 minutes, until setting point is reached.

3 Remove the pan from the heat. Pour into warmed sterilised jars, then cover, seal and label.

Bramble (blackberry) jelly

Brambles or blackberries are low in pectin so lemon juice is essential in this recipe. To help the jelly set you can include some unripe red blackberries if you wish. This dark purple jelly is wonderful as a filling for sponge cakes or as an accompaniment to roast lamb.

 1 kg (2 lb 3 oz) blackberries

 150 ml (5 fl oz) water

 Granulated or caster sugar

 Lemon juice

1 Put the blackberries (there's no need to top and tail them) into a large heavy-based pan with the water. Place over a low heat and slowly bring to the boil. Reduce the heat and simmer gently for about 40–60 minutes, until the fruit is very soft.

2 Ladle the fruit and juices into a scalded jelly bag. Strain through the jelly bag overnight.

3 Measure the juice into a large heavy-based pan and to every 600 ml (1 pt) juice, allow 450 g (1 lb) sugar and 2 tablespoons lemon juice.

4 Heat the juice, sugar and lemon juice, and stir over a low heat until the sugar has dissolved completely. Bring to the boil and boil rapidly for about 10 minutes, until setting point is reached.

5 Remove the pan from the heat. Pour into warmed sterilised jars, then cover, seal and label.

Crab apple jelly

*Small, hard crab apples are high in pectin and make one of the best
wild fruit jellies. The colour of the jelly can range from pink to yellow-green,
depending on the variety of crab apple. It is delicious served with scones and
whipped cream or with cold ham or poultry.*

1 Put the crab apples (there's
no need to peel or core them)
into a large heavy-based pan
with the water. Place over a
low heat and slowly bring to
the boil. Reduce the heat and
simmer gently for about
1½ hours, until the fruit is
soft and pulpy.

 2 kg (4 lb 6 oz) crab apples,
cut into quarters

 1.2 litres (2 pt) water

Granulated or caster sugar

2 Ladle the fruit and juices into a scalded jelly bag. Strain through the
jelly bag overnight.

3 Measure the juice into a large heavy-based pan and to every 600 ml
(1 pt) juice, allow 450 g (1 lb) sugar.

4 Heat the juice and sugar, and stir over a low heat until
the sugar has dissolved completely. Bring to the boil
and boil rapidly for about 10–20 minutes, until
setting point is reached.

5 Remove the pan from the heat.
Pour into warmed sterilised jars,
then cover, seal and label.

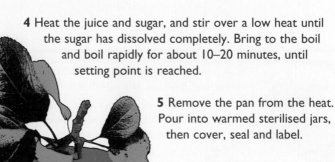

Gooseberry mint jelly

*One of the first fruits of summer, gooseberries make delicious preserves.
For centuries gooseberry jelly has been served with fatty meats such as pork,
lamb and duck, and oily fish such as mackerel, where the gooseberries' tartness
counteracts the richness of the food. Use a mild mint such as apple mint,
pineapple mint or spearmint rather than the strong tasting peppermint.*

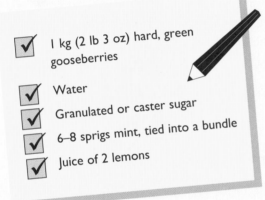

☑ 1 kg (2 lb 3 oz) hard, green gooseberries

☑ Water

☑ Granulated or caster sugar

☑ 6–8 sprigs mint, tied into a bundle

☑ Juice of 2 lemons

1 Put the gooseberries into a large heavy-based pan (there's no need to top and tail them) and just cover with water. Place over a low heat and slowly bring to the boil. Reduce the heat and simmer gently for about 15–20 minutes until the fruit is soft.

2 Ladle the fruit and juices into a scalded jelly bag. Strain through the jelly bag overnight.

3 Measure the juice into a large heavy-based pan and to every 600 ml (1 pt) juice, allow 450 g (1 lb) sugar.

4 Heat the juice, sugar, mint and lemon juice, and stir over a low heat until the sugar has dissolved completely. Bring to the boil and boil rapidly for about 10–20 minutes, until setting point is reached. Remove the mint.

5 Remove the pan from the heat. Pour into warmed sterilised jars, then cover, seal and label.

Herb jelly

You can use a single herb or a mixture of herbs for this savoury jelly. Sage is delicious with pork; parsley with ham; thyme with poultry and rosemary or mint with lamb. Mixed herb jelly is delicious served with fish or with soft cheeses, such as goat's cheese.

1 Put the apples into a large heavy-based pan with the water and herb bundle. Place over a low heat and slowly bring to the boil. Reduce the heat and simmer gently for about 1 hour, until the fruit is soft, stirring from time to time.

2 Add the vinegar and cook for another 5 minutes. Mash the fruit to a pulp.

☑ 1.5 kg (3 lb 5 oz) cooking apples, coarsely chopped

☑ 900 ml (32 fl oz) water

☑ 6–8 sprigs fresh herbs, tied into a bundle

☑ 150 ml (5 fl oz) white malt or white wine vinegar

☑ Granulated or caster sugar

☑ 4 Tbsp chopped fresh herbs

3 Ladle the fruit and juices into a scalded jelly bag. Strain through the jelly bag overnight.

4 Measure the juice into a large heavy-based pan and to every 600 ml (1 pt) juice, allow 450 g (1 lb) sugar.

5 Heat the juice and sugar, and stir over a low heat until the sugar has dissolved completely. Bring to the boil and boil rapidly for about 10 minutes, until setting point is reached.

6 Remove the pan from the heat. Add the chopped herbs and leave to stand for 5–10 minutes, until a skin has formed on the surface. Stir once, pour into warmed sterilised jars, then cover, seal and label.

Medlar jelly

A member of the rose family, medlars are brown pear-shaped fruits with hard, rough skins and have a lightly spicy, rather tart flavour. After picking, the fruit must be allowed to 'blett' – that is, become soft and brown inside before they can be eaten raw. The jelly can be made with ripe or slightly unripe fruit, and is excellent with game or with scones and whipped cream.

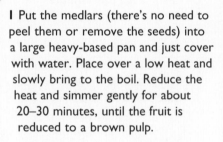

- ☑ 2 kg (4 lb 6 oz) medlars, chopped
- ☑ 1 large lemon
- ☑ 1.75 litres (3 pt) water
- ☑ Granulated or caster sugar
- ☑ Lemon juice, if needed

1 Put the medlars (there's no need to peel them or remove the seeds) into a large heavy-based pan and just cover with water. Place over a low heat and slowly bring to the boil. Reduce the heat and simmer gently for about 20–30 minutes, until the fruit is reduced to a brown pulp.

2 Ladle the fruit and juices into a scalded jelly bag. Strain through the jelly bag overnight.

3 Measure the juice into a large heavy-based pan and to every 600 ml (1 pt) juice, allow 450 g (1 lb) sugar. If using very ripe fruit add 2 tablespoons lemon juice to the pan.

4 Heat the juice, sugar and lemon juice (if using), and stir over a low heat until the sugar has dissolved completely. Bring to the boil and boil rapidly for about 20–25 minutes, until setting point is reached.

5 Remove the pan from the heat. Pour into warmed sterilised jars, then cover, seal and label.

Parsley honey

Parsley has a fresh 'green' vibrant flavour. This is an old country recipe used when honey was in short supply or was difficult to obtain. Parsley honey was a popular substitute for the real thing and looks and tastes like heather honey and can be used wherever you would use honey. It's delicious spread on scones or toast.

1 Wash the parsley well and dry thoroughly. Chop it roughly, including the stalks, and put into a large heavy-based pan with the water. Place over a low heat and slowly bring to the boil. Boil steadily for about 30 minutes, until the liquid is reduced to 600 ml (1 pt).

150 g (5½ oz) fresh parsley

850 ml (1½ pt) water

450 g (1 lb) granulated or caster sugar

½ tsp white malt or white wine vinegar, or juice of 1 small lemon

2 Strain the mixture into a clean pan and add the sugar. Heat gently until the sugar has dissolved completely, then bring to the boil. Cook steadily for about 20 minutes, until clear and syrupy, like thin honey. Stir in the vinegar or lemon juice.

3 Remove from the heat. Pour into warmed sterilised jars, then cover, seal and label. The mixture will set overnight.

Quince jelly

Wonderfully perfumed quinces are hard and inedible when raw but delectable when cooked, when the flesh becomes deep pink. As this jelly cooks it will fill the house with a wonderful aroma. Add a spoonful of quince jelly to apple pies or crumbles before cooking or serve with roast meats and game. If using very ripe fruit use the smaller amount of water and the maximum if the fruit is hard.

 1 kg (2 lb 3 oz) quinces

 900 ml–1.5 litres (1½–2¾ pt) water

 Granulated or caster sugar

1 Wash the quinces and scrub away the greyish down (there's no need to peel or core them). Cut them roughly into pieces and put them into a large heavy-based pan with the water. Place over a low heat and slowly bring to the boil. Reduce the heat and simmer gently for about 40–50 minutes, until the fruit is reduced to a pulp.

2 Ladle the fruit and juices into a scalded jelly bag. Strain through the jelly bag overnight.

3 Measure the juice into a large heavy-based pan and to every 600 ml (1 pt) juice, allow 450 g (1 lb) sugar.

4 Heat the juice and sugar and stir over a low heat until the sugar has dissolved completely. Bring to the boil and boil rapidly for about 15 minutes, until setting point is reached.

5 Remove the pan from the heat. Pour into warmed sterilised jars, then cover, seal and label.

Redcurrant and rosemary jelly

Scarlet translucent redcurrant jelly is delicious with game and roast lamb.
Rosemary is added to the traditional recipe to give a lovely aromatic flavour
to the sweet jelly. Add a spoonful to gravy for lamb or game for extra flavour.

1 Put the redcurrants (there's no need to remove the stalks) into a large heavy-based pan with the water. Place over a low heat and slowly bring to the boil. Reduce the heat and simmer gently for about 20–30 minutes, until the fruit is very soft.

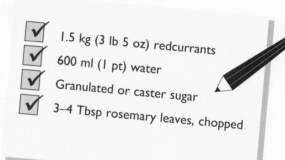

- ☑ 1.5 kg (3 lb 5 oz) redcurrants
- ☑ 600 ml (1 pt) water
- ☑ Granulated or caster sugar
- ☑ 3–4 Tbsp rosemary leaves, chopped

2 Ladle the fruit and juices into a scalded jelly bag. Strain through the jelly bag overnight.

3 Measure the juice into a large heavy-based pan and to every 600 ml (1 pt) juice, allow 450 g (1 lb) sugar. Heat the juice and sugar and stir over a low heat until the sugar has dissolved completely.

4 Add the rosemary, bring to the boil and boil rapidly for about 10–20 minutes, until setting point is reached.

5 Remove the pan from the heat. Pour into warmed sterilised jars, then cover, seal and label.

Rowan jelly

Rowanberries are the fruit of the Mountain Ash tree. The orange red berries make a tangy jelly with a hint of bitterness, which is traditionally served as an accompaniment to game, particularly venison. It is also delicious with other meats.

✓ 1 kg (2 lb 3 oz) rowanberries

✓ 300 ml (11 fl oz) water

✓ Granulated or caster sugar

I Put the rowanberries (there's no need to peel and core them) into a large heavy-based pan with the water. Place over a low heat and slowly bring to the boil. Reduce the heat and simmer gently for about 30–40 minutes, until the fruit is very soft.

2 Ladle the fruit and juices into a scalded jelly bag. Strain through the jelly bag overnight.

3 Measure the juice into a large heavy-based pan and to every 600 ml (1 pt) juice, allow 450 g (1 lb) sugar.

4 Heat the juice and sugar, and stir over a low heat until the sugar has dissolved completely. Bring to the boil and boil rapidly for about 10–15 minutes, until setting point is reached.

5 Remove the pan from the heat. Pour into warmed sterilised jars, then cover, seal and label.

Seville orange marmalade

Bitter or Seville oranges are highly scented with gloriously fragrant aromatic peel and astringent juice. The fruit inspired the creation of Curaçao liqueur and orange marmalade. Sweet orange juice and peel would be too insipid and lack the depth of flavour needed for this superb marmalade.

1 Cut the oranges in half and squeeze out the juice and pips. Scoop out the flesh and reserve. Cut away any thick white pith from the peel and finely shred the peel with a sharp knife.

✓ 1.5 kg (3 lb 5 oz) Seville oranges, scrubbed

✓ Juice of 2 lemons

✓ 3.4 litres (6 pt) water

✓ 3 kg (6 lb 10 oz) granulated or caster sugar, warmed in a very low oven

2 Put the shredded peel, orange and lemon juices, muslin bag and water into a large heavy-based pan. Place over a low heat and slowly bring to the boil. Reduce the heat and simmer gently for 1½–2 hours, until the peel is tender.

3 Stir in the warmed sugar until completely dissolved and then bring to the boil. Boil rapidly for about 15 minutes, until setting point is reached.

4 Remove the pan from the heat. Skim off any scum from the surface and leave to stand for 10–20 minutes. Stir once, pour into warmed sterilised jars, then cover, seal and label.

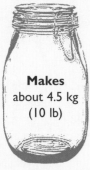

Makes
about 4.5 kg
(10 lb)

Grapefruit and lemon marmalade

Made from two tartly refreshing citrus fruits, this marmalade has a wonderful fruity flavour. The citrus zing and sharp fragrance of tangy grapefruit and lemons make a peppy preserve. Citrus fruits may be waxed to protect them from bruising during shipping and as the peel is used, it is best to use organically grown lemons and limes, which are unwaxed. Wash the fruit, scrubbing the skin to remove any dirt or bacteria on the surface and dry well.

 I kg (2 lb 3 oz) grapefruit, scrubbed

 450 g (1 lb) lemons, scrubbed

 1.7 litres (3 pt) water

 1.5 kg (3 lb 5 oz) granulated or caster sugar, warmed in a very low oven

1 Place the fruit in boiling water for 3 minutes (this makes the fruit easier to peel). Remove from the water and peel with a potato peeler. Cut the peel into fine shreds and put into a large heavy-based pan.

2 Remove the pith from the fruit and chop the flesh roughly. Add the flesh to the pan together with any juice from the fruit.

3 Place the pith and pips in a muslin bag and add to the pan with the water. Place over a low heat and slowly bring to the boil. Reduce the heat and simmer gently for 1½–2 hours, until the peel is tender. Remove the pan from the heat and squeeze the muslin bag into the mixture before discarding it.

4 Stir in the warmed sugar until completely dissolved and then bring to the boil. Boil rapidly for about 10–15 minutes, until setting point is reached.

5 Remove the pan from the heat. Skim off any scum from the surface and leave to stand for 10–20 minutes. Stir once, pour into warmed sterilised jars, then cover, seal and label.

Makes
about 2.5 kg
(5 lb 8 oz)

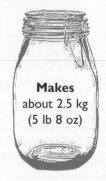

Lime marmalade

Limes make a very tasty marmalade. They have less juice than lemons so lemon juice is added to the recipe. Choose limes that are firm and heavy for their size, with deep green shiny skin when their sharp, tart flavour is at its best.

1 Place the limes in boiling water for 3 minutes (this makes the fruit easier to peel). Remove the rind from the limes with a potato peeler and cut into fine shreds.

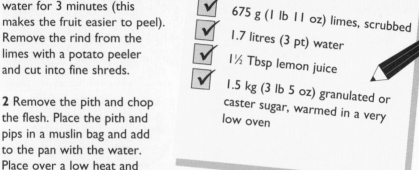

☑ 675 g (1 lb 11 oz) limes, scrubbed
☑ 1.7 litres (3 pt) water
☑ 1½ Tbsp lemon juice
☑ 1.5 kg (3 lb 5 oz) granulated or caster sugar, warmed in a very low oven

2 Remove the pith and chop the flesh. Place the pith and pips in a muslin bag and add to the pan with the water. Place over a low heat and slowly bring to the boil. Reduce the heat and simmer gently for 1–1½ hours, until the peel is tender. Remove the pan from the heat and squeeze the muslin bag into the mixture before discarding it.

3 Stir in the warm sugar and lemon juice and cook over a low heat, stirring all the time until completely dissolved. Bring to the boil and boil rapidly for about 10–15 minutes, until setting point is reached.

4 Remove the pan from the heat. Skim off any foam from the surface and leave to stand for 10 minutes. Stir once, pour into warmed sterilised jars, then cover, seal and label.

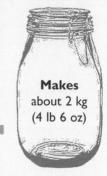

Makes
about 2 kg
(4 lb 6 oz)

Fruit butters and curds

Fruit butters and curds are traditional preserves that were made originally to use up a glut of fruit and were intended to be eaten fairly quickly, as they don't keep as well as jams. Delicious spread on bread and butter, they also make excellent fillings for tarts and cakes.

Equipment

A heavy-based or double saucepan or heatproof bowl.

A fine sieve to remove any lumps.

Sterilised glass jars (see page 15) and metal or plastic covers or lids. Fruit butters are not covered with waxed discs but with airtight metal or plastic lids only.

Ingredients

Almost any fruit is suitable. Homemade lemon curd made from fresh lemons has a much better flavour than commercial brands. Lemons have a refreshingly sharp citrus flavour. Choose thin-skinned fruits (those with thicker peel will have less flesh and therefore be less juicy) that are heavy for their size and bright yellow. Avoid any that are tinged with green as they're not fully ripe and will be very acidic. Use unwaxed citrus fruits if possible; otherwise the fruit must be well scrubbed under hot running water, to remove the protective waxy coating of fungicide. Use a potato peeler to remove the rind in thin strips and don't include the white pith as this is very bitter.

Limes are oval or round in shape with green flesh and skin and are more fragrant than lemons. Choose limes that are firm and heavy for their size, with deep green shiny skin. Use unwaxed fruits if possible.

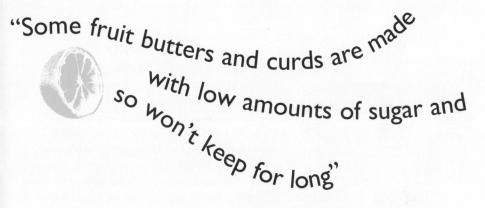

"Some fruit butters and curds are made with low amounts of sugar and so won't keep for long"

Some fruit butters and curds are made with low amounts of sugar and so will not keep for very long. Use fresh eggs, but not newly laid: about two days old is ideal. This is because very fresh eggs have a high moisture content, which will prevent the mixture from thickening. Eggs with deep-coloured yolks are best for lemon curd. Use unsalted butter otherwise the curd will be slightly salty.

Cooking

The ingredients are cooked together until the mixture becomes stiff, thick and smooth. Mixtures containing egg yolks are cooked in a double saucepan or heatproof bowl over a pan of simmering (but not boiling) water to prevent the egg from over cooking and the mixture from curdling and separating. The water must not touch the base of the bowl as too much heat will be transferred and it will cause the mixture to boil, spoiling the curd. When cool, the curd becomes thick enough to spread.

Check that the sugar has dissolved completely. The mixture should be thick enough to coat the back of a spoon.

As a general guide, fruit curd is ready when a spoon drawn across the surface of the mixture leaves a clean line. Fruit butter is ready when no free liquid is visible and the surface is creamy.

It is difficult to estimate how much preserve a recipe will make, as this depends on how juicy the fruit is. As a general guide, 450 g (1 lb) sugar should make about 750 g (1 lb 11 oz) fruit butter or curd.

Spoon the mixture into sterilised jars (see page 15) right up to the top as the mixture will shrink a little as it cools. The jars are then sealed and labelled in the same way as for jam (see page 23). The jars must be stored in the refrigerator and eaten within two to three weeks. Once opened the curds or butters should be eaten with a few days.

What can go wrong?
Curdling (separating) occurs in preserves made with eggs if the mixture becomes too hot. The mixture should be cooked very slowly, stirring continuously in a double saucepan or bowl over a pan of simmering water so that the mixture doesn't come into contact with direct heat. If the mixture curdles remove from the heat immediately and whisk vigorously to amalgamate the mixture again. Continue to whisk until thick.

Mould occurs if the preserve is kept in a warm or damp place. Fruit butters and curds should be kept in the refrigerator and eaten within three weeks. Inspect regularly for signs of mould.

Apple butter

Cooking apples have a sharp, tart flavour and retain their shape well during cooking. Apple butter is lightly spiced and is delicious spread on scones, bread or toast, and also as a filling for sponge cakes. Using cider instead of water produces a more pronounced apple flavour.

1 Put the apples (including cores and peel) into a large heavy-based pan and cover with the water or cider. Bring to the boil and simmer gently for about 30 minutes, until very soft.

 1.5 kg (3 lb 5 oz) cooking apples, coarsely chopped including cores and peel

 1.1 litres (1¾ pt) water or cider

 Pinch ground cloves

 ½ tsp ground cinnamon

 350 g (12½ oz) caster sugar for each 450 g (1 lb) fruit pulp

2 Remove the pan from the heat. Push the mixture through a sieve into a bowl. Weigh the pulp and return it to the pan with the spices.

3 Add the required amount of sugar to the pulp and heat gently, stirring until the sugar has dissolved completely. Bring to the boil and boil steadily until very thick and creamy, stirring frequently.

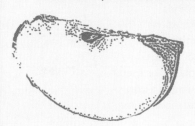

4 Remove the pan from the heat. Pour into warmed sterilised jars, cover with waxed discs and leave until cold before sealing tightly with lids.

Blackberry butter

Wild blackberries are at their best when plump, ripe and full of inky juice. Cultivated blackberries lack the deep flavour of wild berries but are nevertheless still delicious and have the advantage of having fewer seeds than the wild variety. They make a beautiful amethyst-coloured spread that is delicious with scones and cream or as a filling for a plain sponge cake.

 ☑ I kg (2 lb 3 oz) blackberries

 ☑ I kg (2 lb 3 oz) cooking apples, coarsely chopped including cores and peel

☑ Grated zest and juice of 2 lemons

☑ 350 g (12½ oz) caster sugar to every 450 g (1 lb) fruit pulp

1 Put the blackberries and apples (including cores and peel) into a large heavy-based pan with the lemon zest and juice, and slowly bring to the boil. Reduce the heat and simmer gently for about 15 minutes, until very soft.

2 Remove the pan from the heat. Push through a sieve and weigh the pulp. Stir in the required amount of sugar and heat gently until the sugar has dissolved completely.

3 Bring to the boil and cook steadily for about 20 minutes until the mixture is thick and creamy, stirring all the time. The actual cooking time will depend on the ripeness of the fruit.

4 Remove the pan from the heat. Pour into warmed sterilised jars and cover with plastic or metal lids. Label and store in a cool place and use within a month.

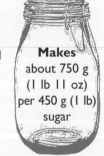

Makes about 750 g (1 lb 11 oz) per 450 g (1 lb) sugar

Plum butter

*You can use any type of plum for this recipe, such as damsons or greengages.
Plums come in dozens of varieties, shapes, sizes and colours. Whether green,
red, deep purple or almost black, they are delicious eaten fresh or baked in
puddings, pies, cakes and jams. The plum is closely related to the almond,
cherry, peach and other species of the genus Prunus.*

Makes
about 750 g
(1 lb 11 oz)
per 450 g (1 lb)
sugar

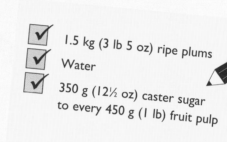

✓ 1.5 kg (3 lb 5 oz) ripe plums
✓ Water
✓ 350 g (12½ oz) caster sugar
to every 450 g (1 lb) fruit pulp

1 Remove the stones from the
plums and put into a large heavy-based pan with just enough water
to cover the fruit. Simmer gently for about 20 minutes, or until very soft.

2 Remove the pan from the heat. Push through a sieve into a bowl.
Weigh the pulp and return it to the pan. Add the required amount of
sugar. Heat gently, stirring until the sugar has dissolved completely.

3 Bring to the boil and cook gently for about 40–60 minutes, until very
thick, stirring frequently.

4 Remove the pan from the heat. Pour into warmed sterilised jars, cover
with waxed discs and leave until cold before sealing tightly with lids.

Quince butter

You may be fortunate to have a quince tree in your garden, but if not, quinces can be found in ethnic food stores and some large supermarkets in the autumn. This preserve is delicious with cheese and crackers or bread and butter, or as an accompaniment to roast pork. Wash the quinces and scrub off the grey down before you start.

Makes
about 750 g
(1 lb 11 oz)
per 450 g (1 lb)
sugar

☑ 1 kg (2 lb 3 oz) quinces, peeled and cored weight

☑ 450 ml (16 fl oz) water

☑ 450 g (1 lb) caster sugar to every 450 g (1 lb) fruit pulp

☑ 3 Tbsp lemon juice to every 450 g (1 lb) fruit pulp

☑ Knob of unsalted butter

1 Cut the quinces into small pieces and place in a large heavy-based pan with the water. Bring to the boil, then reduce the heat. Simmer gently for about 20–40 minutes, or until very soft.

2 Remove the pan from the heat. Push through a sieve into a bowl. Weigh the pulp and return it to the pan. Add the required amount of sugar and lemon juice. Heat gently, stirring until the sugar has dissolved completely, then bring to the boil and cook gently for about 40 minutes, until very thick, stirring frequently.

3 Remove the pan from the heat. Pour into warmed sterilised jars, cover with waxed discs and cover with plastic or metal lids immediately.

Apricot curd

Fresh, golden, juicy apricots can vary in colour from pale yellow to deep orange. They make a delectable spread for fresh bread and butter, and scones. Add a few of the cracked stones to the mixture for a subtle almond flavour but remember to remove them before potting.

1 Put the apricots into a medium pan with very little water and cook for about 15–20 minutes, until soft. Push the mixture through a nylon sieve into a heatproof bowl. Stir in the sugar, lemon zest and juice and butter.

☑ 225 g (8 oz) fresh ripe apricots, cut in half

☑ 225 g (8 oz) caster sugar

☑ Grated zest and juice of 1 lemon

☑ 50 g (2 oz) unsalted butter, diced

☑ 2 eggs, beaten

2 Place the bowl over a pan of simmering (but not boiling) water and cook, stirring until the sugar has dissolved.

3 Stir in the eggs and continue stirring for about 20 minutes, until the mixture thickens enough to coat the back of a wooden spoon. Be careful not to cook for too long as the mixture will thicken more as it cools.

Makes about 450 g (1 lb)

4 Remove the bowl and pan from the heat. Pour into warmed sterilised jars, cover with waxed discs and leave until cold before sealing tightly with cellophane covers or lids.

5 Label and store in a cool place and use within a month.

Gooseberry curd ● ● ● ● ●

Hard, bright green gooseberries are one of the first fruits of the year. They are sharp and sour tasting when raw, but their acidity is transformed by cooking them with sugar. In wet weather, gooseberries exude more liquid so may need cooking for a little longer.

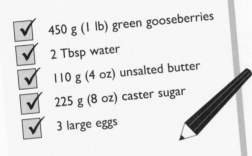

- ✓ 450 g (1 lb) green gooseberries
- ✓ 2 Tbsp water
- ✓ 110 g (4 oz) unsalted butter
- ✓ 225 g (8 oz) caster sugar
- ✓ 3 large eggs

1 Put the gooseberries into a large heavy-based pan (there's no need to top and tail them) with the water. Bring to the boil and simmer gently for about 15 minutes, until very soft.

2 Remove the pan from the heat. Push the mixture through a sieve into a bowl and reserve.

3 Put the butter and sugar into a separate large heatproof bowl, place over a pan of simmering (but not boiling) water and stir to dissolve the sugar. When the butter has melted and the sugar has dissolved completely, stir in the reserved gooseberry purée.

4 Beat the eggs lightly and stir into the warm mixture. Cook over the simmering water for about 20–30 minutes, stirring, until the mixture thickens enough to coat the back of a spoon.

5 Remove the bowl and pan from the heat. Pour into warmed sterilised jars, cover with waxed discs and leave until cold before sealing tightly with lids.

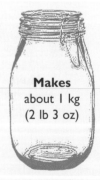

Makes
about 1 kg
(2 lb 3 oz)

Lemon curd

This tastes so much nicer than the commercial variety and has a lovely fresh lemon flavour with just a hint of sharpness. Some lemons may be waxed to protect them from bruising during shipping. As the zest is used, it is best to use organically grown lemons and limes, which are unwaxed. Alternatively, scrub the fruit very well in warm water to remove the waxy coating.

1 Put the lemon zest, juice, sugar and butter into a heatproof bowl. Place over a pan of simmering (but not boiling) water and stir to dissolve the sugar.

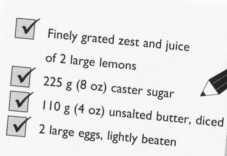

✔ Finely grated zest and juice of 2 large lemons

✔ 225 g (8 oz) caster sugar

✔ 110 g (4 oz) unsalted butter, diced

✔ 2 large eggs, lightly beaten

2 Stir in the eggs and continue stirring for about 20 minutes, until the mixture thickens enough to coat the back of a wooden spoon. Be careful not to cook for too long as the mixture will thicken more as it cools.

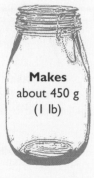

Makes
about 450 g
(1 lb)

3 Remove the bowl and pan from the heat. Pour into warmed sterilised jars, cover with waxed discs and leave until cold before sealing tightly with cellophane covers or lids.

4 Store in a cool place and use within a month.

Pumpkin curd

The onset of autumn brings with it the annual appearance of a colourful array of pumpkins ranging in colour from pale gold to deep, dark green. This curd makes an unusual filling for a sponge cake and is also good spread on scones and bread.

 450 g (1 lb) pumpkin, peeled and seeded weight

 2 large eggs

 450 g (1 lb) caster sugar

 Juice of 2 large lemons

1 Cut the pumpkin flesh into pieces and put into a large sieve or metal colander over a pan of boiling water. Cover and steam for 30 minutes, then mash to a purée. Transfer to a heatproof bowl.

2 Beat the eggs lightly and stir into the warm purée with the sugar and lemon juice.

3 Cook over a pan of simmering (but not boiling) water for about 20–30 minutes, stirring, until the mixture thickens enough to coat the back of a spoon.

4 Remove the bowl and pan from the heat. Pour into warmed sterilised jars, cover with waxed discs and leave until cold before sealing tightly with lids.

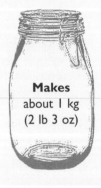

Makes about 1 kg (2 lb 3 oz)

Damson cheese

*Damsons are indigestible when raw, but the sharp tasting fruit
is transformed during cooking and makes wonderful preserves.
Serve this preserve sliced with roast lamb or beef, or as a dessert
with whipped cream.*

1 Put the whole damsons into
a large heavy-based pan with
the water. Bring to the boil
and simmer gently for about
30 minutes, until very soft.

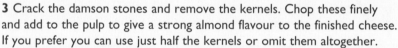

1.3 kg (3 lb) damsons

150–250 ml (5–9 fl oz) water

450 g (1 lb) caster sugar for
each 450 g (1 lb) fruit pulp

2 Push the mixture through
a sieve into a bowl. Weigh
the pulp and return it to
the pan.

3 Crack the damson stones and remove the kernels. Chop these finely
and add to the pulp to give a strong almond flavour to the finished cheese.
If you prefer you can use just half the kernels or omit them altogether.

4 Add the required amount of sugar to the pulp and heat gently, stirring
until the sugar has dissolved completely. Bring to the boil and cook gently
for about 1 hour or until very thick, stirring frequently.

5 Remove the bowl and pan from the heat. Pour into
warmed sterilised jars, cover with
waxed discs and leave until cold
before sealing tightly with lids.

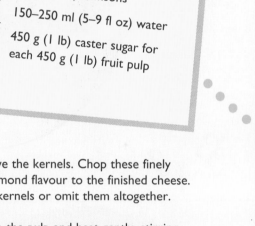

Chutney

Chutney is a piquantly sweet/sour condiment made from fruits and vegetables and may range from mildly spiced to very hot. Chutney will pep up bland foods (add a spoonful to a baked potato for instance) into a tasty meal. It keeps very well and the flavour actually improves if the chutney is left for at least two months before opening the jar.

Equipment

Use a stainless steel or anodised aluminium pan – never brass, copper, old-fashioned aluminium or iron – as vinegar will react with and corrode these metals and also taint the chutney.

A wide funnel is useful when filling the jars, but a jug or a small ladle can be used instead.

Kilner (Mason) jars are ideal for storing homemade preserves and are available in a range of sizes. A Kilner jar is a glass jar which has a lid in two sections to ensure an airtight seal. Originally a glass disc sat on top of the jar and was then secured in place with a metal screw band which contains a rubber seal. Nowadays both sections of the lid are usually made from metal. The original Kilner jar is sometimes mistaken for the more widely available glass jar with a rubber seal and a metal hinge, which when closed forms an airtight seal. These jars can be used instead of a Kilner jar.

Lids must be vinegar-proof, i.e. lined with plastic. Plastic lids from coffee jars are perfect. Cellophane covers are not suitable as lids must also be completely airtight or the chutney will dry out as the vinegar evaporates. If you only have metal lids, line them with a disc of waxed paper first.

Ingredients

Choose fresh-looking, firm, ripe fruits
and vegetables. Fruits and vegetables
are usually finely chopped or minced.
Dried fruits are often included to
add sweetness.

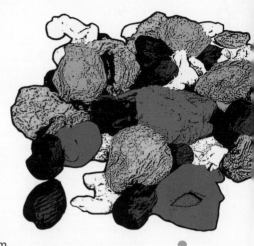

Dried fruits include currants, raisins
(muscatel raisins are the finest as they
are plump and full of rich sweet flavour,
although they are more expensive) and
sultanas (dried white grapes, paler than
currants and raisins), which all come from
different types of grapes; prunes are dried plums and these glistening
black fruits have a splendid flavour and moist texture; dates are the fruit
of a palm tree and have a rich sweet flavour; figs flourish in hot countries
and, in the past, cooked figs were used as sweeteners in place of
expensive sugar and are still used for this purpose today in North Africa
and the Middle East. The best are Smyrna-type figs, which have a whitish
coating of crystallised natural sugars. The best dried apricots are those
from the Hunza valley in Kashmir and from Afghanistan and Turkey.
The wild fruits are left on the trees to dry before they are picked. Hunza
apricots, it has to be said, do look uninviting; small, round, hard and beige in
colour, they look like little stones, totally unlike fresh, plump, vivid orange
apricots. They need to be soaked and cooked before cooking but their
flavour is unsurpassable – deep and rich with a hint of toffee.

Some fruits, such as prunes and apricots, need soaking before use,
although no-soak varieties are now widely available. You can use either
in the recipes, but if using fruits which require soaking you can make
these even more delicious by soaking in orange juice, apple juice, wine
or tea, instead of water.

Newcomers to the dried fruit market are cranberries, blueberries and a variety of exotic fruits such as papaya and mango. These don't need to be soaked before use and are used in the same way as currants, raisins, etc.

Vinegar is a key ingredient as it acts as a preservative and also contributes to the flavour. It is important to use good-quality vinegar with an acetic acid content of at least 5%; never use anything labelled 'non-brewed condiment'. The type of vinegar you use will give a different flavour to the chutney or pickle. Colour is not an indication of strength – malt vinegar, whether white, distilled or brown, is the least expensive and strongest tasting. Brown malt vinegar is used for making rich dark chutneys, while white malt vinegar is better for lighter coloured chutneys so that the pale colour is not spoiled. Cider vinegar is golden coloured with a delicate flavour best suited to fruit chutneys. Wine vinegar can be either red or white, and red has the stronger flavour. It is not as harsh as malt vinegar and also requires less time to soften the chutney after potting.

Sugar may be white or brown and the latter will give a darker colour and stronger flavour. Black treacle is sometimes included to give extra flavour.

Spices are an important ingredient and are included to give the chutney the necessary savoury spicy flavour and should be as fresh as possible. Using old stale spices that have been in the cupboard for a long time won't flavour the chutney at all, so make sure they are freshly bought. Spices can be whole or ground. Whole spices give a better flavour, as the volatile oils are preserved during storage. These should be bruised (beaten lightly with a rolling pin or other heavy object) to release their flavour, then tied in a piece of muslin so they can be removed easily before potting.

Popular spices for chutney and pickles

Allspice is not a blend of spices as many people wrongly think but is a spice in its own right. It has a highly aromatic flavour often described as a combination of cinnamon, clove, nutmeg and pepper. Allspice is available as whole dried berries or ready ground.

Cardamom is the dried, unopened fruit of a plant native to south India. It has a warm, spicy, sweet, slightly lemony flavour and is sold whole in pods, as small blackish brown seeds and ready ground. The pods and seeds should be lightly crushed before using to release the flavour.

Cayenne pepper is a red, fiery hot spice ground from the pod and seeds of dried chillies and should be used sparingly. Just a pinch is all that's usually required.

Cinnamon has a warm sweet fragrance and is sold as sticks or quills and as a powder. You can try to grind your own cinnamon from the bark but it's difficult to get it fine enough. It's best to buy ground cinnamon in small quantities because the freshness and flavour quickly disappear.

Cloves are the dried flower buds of a tree in Indonesia. Cloves have a pungent spicy flavour and should be used sparingly.

Coriander has a warm aromatic, slightly nutty flavour with a hint of orange and is sold whole as seeds and ready ground.

Cumin is sold as whole seeds or ready ground and imparts a warm, slightly sweet spiciness to chutneys.

Ginger can be used as the fresh root, crystallised or candied in syrup or dried and ground. It adds a touch of heat and has a warm fragrant aroma and flavour.

Juniper berries have a bittersweet, slightly resinous flavour and should be lightly crushed or bruised before using to release the volatile flavouring oils.

Mace is the outer lacy covering of the nutmeg. It is sold either in blades or ground and adds a mild nutmeg flavour.

Mixed spice is a commercial blend of sweet spices, including cinnamon and coriander seed. It adds a warm spicy note.

Mustard seed has a fresh clean fresh aroma and pungent, sharp flavour.

Nutmeg has a warm spicy flavour. Buy whole nutmeg and grate it as you need it. Avoid using ready-ground nutmeg, which quickly loses its flavour.

Turmeric is the root or rhizome of a member of the ginger family and adds a pungent flavour and deep orange-yellow colour. It is sold ready ground.

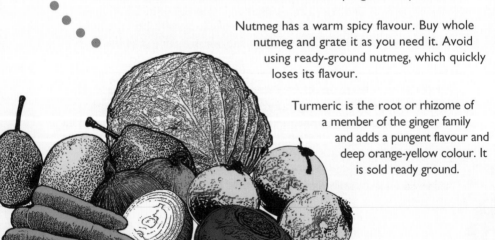

Cooking

It's a good idea to open the kitchen windows and close the kitchen door, or the pungent smell of boiling vinegar will permeate throughout the house.

Chutney is cooked slowly for a long time to give a good rich flavour and dark colour. The mixture is stirred with a wooden spoon from time to time to prevent it sticking to the pan and burning. After cooking for about an hour, the chutney will need stirring constantly. It should have a spoonable consistency, but it will also thicken a little more as it cools. Depending on the recipe, the mixture will need cooking for one to three hours, but be careful not to cook it for too long or the sugar will caramelise.

The texture may be chunky or smooth, depending on the recipe. Chutneys do not set with pectin; it is the evaporation of the vinegar that results in the correct texture, as chutneys will set firmer when cold. To test when the chutney is cooked make a channel across the surface with a wooden spoon: if the impression lasts for a few seconds and does not fill up with vinegar it is ready. Taste the chutney but remember that chutney needs time in the jar to mellow to allow the acidity to soften and the flavours to develop.

The hot chutney is poured into warmed sterilised jars right up to the brim and covered while still hot. Chutney will taste better if left to mature for at least three months before eating and will keep in a cool, dry, dark place for two to three years. Once opened store in the refrigerator.

What can go wrong?

Raw flavour is caused by not cooking the mixture sufficiently. The longer chutney is cooked, the richer and mellower the flavour will be.

Apple, apricot and cardamom chutney

This combination of flavour is particularly delicious with pork, ham or sausages. Cardamom seeds are very fragrant and impart a highly aromatic, warm citrus-like flavour with subtle floral tones. Light muscovado sugar adds a rich taste with a hint of molasses.

 450 g (1 lb) onions, peeled and finely chopped

 300 ml (11 fl oz) white malt vinegar

 1 kg (2 lb 3 oz) cooking apples, peeled and cored weight

 2 tsp cardamom seeds, crushed

 350 g (12½ oz) light muscovado sugar

 110 g (4 oz) ready-to-eat dried apricots, roughly chopped

 Salt and pepper

1 Put the onions and half the vinegar into a large heavy-based pan and bring to the boil. Reduce the heat and simmer gently for 10 minutes.

2 Cut the apples into small pieces and add to the pan with the remaining vinegar, cardamom seeds, sugar, dried apricots and a sprinkling of salt and pepper.

3 Stir over a low heat until the sugar has dissolved completely, then increase the heat and simmer steadily, for about 40–60 minutes, stirring occasionally until the mixture is very thick.

4 Remove the pan from the heat. Spoon into hot sterilised jars, seal and label.

5 Leave to mature for up to 3 months in a cool, dry, dark place.

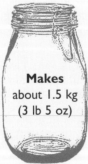

Makes
about 1.5 kg
(3 lb 5 oz)

Apricot and onion chutney

Dried apricots have a more pronounced flavour than fresh ones, but either can be used. This is a mild-tasting chutney that goes well with all kinds of meat and poultry and pies as well as cheese.

1 Put all the ingredients, except the sugar, into a large heavy-based pan and bring to the boil. Reduce the heat and simmer for about 45 minutes, until the mixture is thick and pulpy. Remove from the heat and stir in the sugar until completely dissolved.

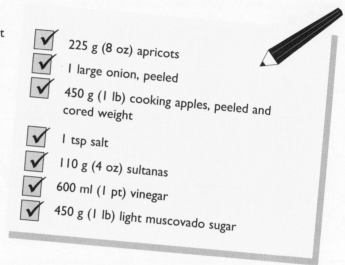

✔ 225 g (8 oz) apricots

✔ 1 large onion, peeled

✔ 450 g (1 lb) cooking apples, peeled and cored weight

✔ 1 tsp salt

✔ 110 g (4 oz) sultanas

✔ 600 ml (1 pt) vinegar

✔ 450 g (1 lb) light muscovado sugar

Makes about 1.5 kg (3 lb 5 oz)

2 Return to a low heat and stir well, then increase the heat and simmer steadily, for about 20 minutes, stirring occasionally until the mixture is very thick.

3 Remove the pan from the heat. Spoon into hot sterilised jars, seal and label.

Autumn chutney

This recipe is an ideal way to use up a glut of autumn fruits. You can vary the proportions of fruit, according to what you have available, as long as the total weight of fruit remains the same. For example you could use blackberries instead of the apricots, or use half the amount of pears and use plums to make up the weight.

 450 g (1 lb) onions, peeled and finely chopped

 300 ml (11 fl oz) white malt vinegar

 450 g (1 lb) cooking apples, peeled and cored weight

 450 g (1 lb) pears, peeled and cored weight

 110 g (4 oz) dried apricots, chopped

 350 g (12½ oz) light muscovado sugar

 Salt and pepper

1 Put the onions and half the vinegar into a large heavy-based pan and bring to the boil. Reduce the heat and simmer gently for 10 minutes.

2 Cut the apples and pears into small pieces, and add to the pan with the remaining vinegar, apricots, sugar and a sprinkling of salt and pepper.

3 Stir over a low heat until the sugar has dissolved completely, then increase the heat and simmer steadily, for about 40–60 minutes, stirring occasionally until the mixture is very thick.

4 Remove the pan from the heat. Spoon into hot sterilised jars, seal and label.

5 Leave to mature for at least 3 months in a cool, dry, dark place.

Makes
about 1.8 kg
(4 lb)

Beetroot chutney

Beetroot has a wonderful colour, and when combined with onions and apples, makes a tasty chutney that's ideal with cheese and cold meats. It is also good with poultry.

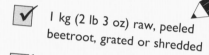

Makes
about 2.5 kg
(5 lb 8 oz)

✔ I kg (2 lb 3 oz) raw, peeled beetroot, grated or shredded

✔ 450 g (I lb) onions, peeled and chopped

✔ 675 g (I lb 8 oz) apples, peeled and chopped

✔ 450 g (I lb) seedless raisins

✔ I.I litres (1¾ pt) malt vinegar

✔ I tsp mixed pickling spices

✔ I kg (2 lb 3 oz) white or brown sugar

I Put all the ingredients in a large heavy-based pan and slowly bring to the boil. Reduce the heat and simmer gently for about I hour, until soft and pulpy.

2 Remove the pan from the heat. Spoon into hot sterilised jars, seal and label.

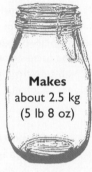

Elderberry chutney

- 450 g (1 lb) elderberries, washed and stalks removed
- 450 g (1 lb) cooking apples, peeled, cored and chopped
- 110 g (4 oz) dried fruit, such as a mix of currants, sultanas, raisins
- 450 g (1 lb) onions, peeled and finely chopped
- 1 tsp salt
- ½ tsp ground ginger
- ½ tsp ground mixed spice
- Pinch ground black pepper
- 300 ml (11 fl oz) malt vinegar
- 350 g (12½ oz) white or brown sugar

A tasty chutney with a fruity flavour. Glossy, black elderberries are the fruit of the elder tree and can be found growing wild in the autumn. They must never be eaten raw as the uncooked berries can cause nausea and/ or vomiting and so are always cooked. The easiest way to remove the berries from the stalks is to strip them using the prongs of a fork.

1 Put the elderberries, apples, dried fruit and onions into a large heavy-based pan with the salt, spices, pepper and one third of the vinegar. Bring to the boil, then reduce the heat and simmer very gently for about 1 hour, until the fruit is soft, stirring from time to time to prevent the mixture sticking and burning.

2 Remove from the heat and stir in the sugar and remaining vinegar. When the sugar has dissolved completely, return to the heat and bring to the boil. Boil steadily for about 30–40 minutes, until thick.

3 Remove the pan from the heat. Spoon into hot sterilised jars, seal and label.

Makes about 1.8 kg (4 lb)

Gooseberry chutney

A well-flavoured fruity spicy chutney that's delicious with rich oily fish, particularly mackerel and smoked salmon. It is also a tasty accompaniment to roast meats and poultry. Cayenne pepper adds a hot spiciness and you can use more or less, as you prefer.

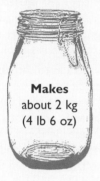

Makes
about 2 kg
(4 lb 6 oz)

 1.5 kg (3 lb 5 oz) green gooseberries, topped and tailed

 450 g (1 lb) onions, peeled and finely chopped

 225 g (8 oz) seedless raisins

 1 Tbsp salt

 1 tsp ground ginger

 ½ tsp cayenne pepper

 350 g (12½ oz) soft brown sugar

 600 ml (1 pt) white vinegar

1 Put all the ingredients in a large heavy-based pan over a low heat and slowly bring to the boil, stirring until the sugar has dissolved completely.

2 Reduce the heat and simmer gently, for about 1–2 hours, stirring frequently until thick.

3 Remove the pan from the heat. Spoon into hot sterilised jars, seal and label.

Green tomato chutney

Green tomatoes have a firm texture and a sharp flavour with just a hint of tomato. A recipe that was popular with the Victorians, who regarded this as an ideal accompaniment to cheeses and cold meats.

 1.5 kg (3 lb 5 oz) green tomatoes, sliced

 450 g (1 lb) cooking apples, peeled, cored and chopped

 675 g (1 lb 8 oz) shallots or onions, peeled and finely chopped

 2 cloves garlic, peeled (optional)

 225 g (8 oz) raisins

 1 tsp salt

 ½ tsp cayenne pepper

 15 g (½ oz) fresh root ginger, bruised

 600 ml (1 pt) vinegar

 450 g (1 lb) soft brown sugar

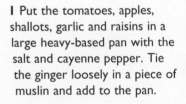

1 Put the tomatoes, apples, shallots, garlic and raisins in a large heavy-based pan with the salt and cayenne pepper. Tie the ginger loosely in a piece of muslin and add to the pan.

2 Stir in one third of the vinegar and cook gently over a low heat for about 1 hour, until the vegetables and fruit are soft, stirring from time to time.

3 Remove from the heat and stir in the sugar and remaining vinegar. When the sugar has dissolved completely, return to the heat and bring to the boil. Reduce the heat and simmer gently for 1–1½ hours, until thick.

4 Remove the pan from the heat. Spoon into hot sterilised jars, seal and label.

Makes
about 2 kg
(4 lb 6 oz)

Ripe tomato chutney

There are lots of varieties of tomatoes and any can be used to make this red chutney, which has a different flavour from chutney made with green tomatoes and looks and tastes very appetising. To ripen home-grown tomatoes, place them in a paper bag with a ripe tomato and keep at room temperature.

1 Put all the ingredients except the sugar, sultanas, salt and pepper into a large heavy-based pan. Bring to the boil, then reduce the heat and simmer steadily, for about 20 minutes, stirring occasionally until thick.

Makes
about 2.5 kg
(5 lb 8 oz)

 1 kg (2 lb 3 oz) firm ripe tomatoes, skinned and chopped

 450 g (1 lb) onions, peeled and finely chopped

 450 g (1 lb) cooking apples, peeled and cored weight, finely chopped

 450 ml (16 fl oz) vinegar

 1 tsp ground ginger

 1 tsp ground mixed spice

 350 g (12½ oz) white or brown sugar

 300 g (10½ oz) sultanas

 Salt and pepper

2 Remove from the heat and stir in the sugar until dissolved completely. Add the sultanas and season to taste. Stir well, over a low heat, then increase the heat and simmer steadily, for about 20 minutes, stirring occasionally until the mixture is very thick.

3 Remove the pan from the heat. Spoon into hot sterilised jars, seal and label.

Pear and orange chutney

There are over 5,000 varieties of pears and any can be used in this recipe, although slightly underripe pears are best for cooking. Oranges add a refreshing sweet tartness to this chutney. It is particulary good with duck and other rich tasting meats.

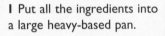

 1.5 kg (3 lb 5 oz) hard pears, peeled and cored weight, roughly chopped

 1 large onion, peeled and finely chopped

 225 g (8 oz) seedless raisins

 350 g (12½ oz) light muscovado sugar

 Finely grated zest and juice of 2 oranges

 1 tsp ground ginger

 Pinch of ground cloves

1 Put all the ingredients into a large heavy-based pan.

2 Stir well over a low heat until the sugar has dissolved completely. Bring to the boil then reduce the heat and simmer gently, for 1–2 hours, stirring occasionally, until thick.

3 Remove the pan from the heat. Spoon into hot sterilised jars, seal and label.

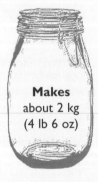

Makes
about 2 kg
(4 lb 6 oz)

Rhubarb chutney

Young succulent stems of rhubarb have a refreshingly tart flavour. This tasty chutney is excellent with fatty meats such as pork or duck when its sharp fresh taste will cut through the richness of the meat

Makes
about 2 kg
(4 lb 6 oz)

✓ 150 ml (5 fl oz) water

✓ 150 ml (5 fl oz) vinegar

✓ 1 kg (2 lb 3 oz) white or brown sugar

✓ 1 tsp ground allspice

✓ 1 tsp ground ginger

✓ ½ tsp ground cloves

✓ 1.5 kg (3 lb 5 oz) rhubarb, cut into 2.5-cm pieces

✓ 450 g (1 lb) sultanas or raisins

1 Put the water, vinegar, sugar and spices into a large heavy-based pan. Bring to the boil, then reduce the heat and simmer gently for 20 minutes.

2 Add the rhubarb and sultanas or raisins to the vinegar syrup and bring to the boil. Reduce the heat and simmer gently for about 1–2 hours, until thick.

3 Remove the pan from the heat. Spoon into hot sterilised jars, seal and label.

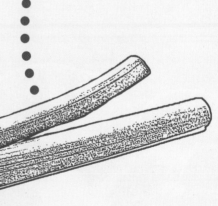

Pickles

Piquant pickles add a kick to all sorts of food — cheeses, cold meats, poultry, meat pies, etc. A spoonful of pickle or a few crisp pickled onions are quick and tasty ways to spice up a plain meal or sandwich.

Equipment

Use a stainless steel or anodised aluminium pan – never brass, copper old-fashioned aluminium or iron – as vinegar will react with and corrode these metals. Modern aluminium pans are anodised – a process which seals the metal – so are fine to use for pickles and chutneys.

Nylon sieves are best as metal could adversely affect the colour and flavour of the finished pickles.

Kilner (Mason) jars are ideal for storing homemade preserves and are available in a range of sizes. A Kilner jar is a glass jar which has a lid in two sections to ensure an airtight seal. Originally a glass disc sat on top of the jar and was then secured in place with a metal screw band which contains a rubber seal. Nowadays both sections of the lid are usually made from metal. The original Kilner jar is sometimes mistaken for the more widely available glass jar with a rubber seal and a metal hinge, which when closed forms an airtight seal. These jars can be used instead of a Kilner jar.

Lids must be vinegar-proof, i.e. lined with plastic. Plastic lids from coffee jars are perfect. If metal comes into contact with the vinegar the lids will rust. Lids must also be airtight or the pickles will dry out. If you only have metal lids, line them with a disc of waxed paper first. Cellophane covers are not suitable as they are too flimsy.

Ingredients

Vinegar is a key ingredient as it acts as a preservative and also contributes to the flavour. It is important to use a good-quality vinegar with an acetic acid content of at least 5%; never use anything labelled 'non-brewed condiment'.

There are many types of vinegar; it can be made from grapes, grains or fruits and each has its own subtly different flavours ranging from mild to strong. The type of vinegar you use will give a different flavour to the pickles. Colour is not an indication of strength – malt vinegar whether white, distilled or brown is the least expensive and strongest tasting. Brown malt vinegar is used for making dark pickles while white malt vinegar is better for lighter coloured and clear pickles, so that the pale colour is not spoiled. Cider vinegar, golden coloured with a delicate flavour, or wine vinegar can also be used, although these are more expensive. White wine vinegar, cider vinegar or white malt vinegar is the best to use for pickled fruits, so that the colour is not impaired.

A commercially made spiced 'pickling vinegar' is also available, which gives a spicy flavour to the finished pickles.

Pickling salt or sea salt is the best to use for brining rather than table salt as the latter has additives, which tend to make the brine cloudy.

Spices are essential to add an interesting and subtle flavour to the pickles. Pickling spice mixes are available and the blends differ greatly according to the manufacturer. The spices usually include allspice, bay leaves, cardamom, cinnamon, cloves, coriander, ginger, mustard seeds and peppercorns and are usually whole or in large pieces. Whole spices give a better flavour, as the volatile oils are preserved during storage. Use spices sparingly as they can be overpowering.

Sugar, white or brown, according to preference, is added to the vinegar and spices to make sweet pickles. These have a sharp but not sour flavour and are excellent with cold meats and poultry.

Fruits and vegetables such as plums, blackberries, onions and beetroot can be pickled. Spices can be added to vary the flavour. Herb sprigs or leaves also add flavour. Bay leaves have a strong aromatic flavour and exude a wonderful aroma when crushed.

Popular vegetables for pickling

Cucumbers for pickling should be young and measure between 5–10 cm (2–4 in), which makes them easier to fit in the jar. Prick them once or twice to allow the flavours to penetrate better.

Mushrooms should be firm and fresh looking with no sign of sweating and the stalk end should be moist, not dry. Small mushrooms, such as button mushrooms are the best to use. Wild mushrooms are excellent but unless you know what you are doing, don't be tempted to pick wild mushrooms, some deadly poisonous mushrooms look remarkably similar to edible varieties! Wild mushrooms are becoming more easily available from specialist shops and local markets and their flavour is far superior to that of cultivated varieties, with each variety having its own very unique flavour.

Onions are probably the most popular vegetable for pickling. The two most commonly used are shallots and pickling or baby onions, which will fit easily into jars. Choose firm onions with unbroken skins; shallots should not have too much evident growth shoot as this indicates that they are past their best.

Red cabbage is a favourite for pickling and should have a tight, compact head that feels heavy for its size. It should look crisp and fresh, with few loose leaves. Discard any outer limp leaves. Remove the core and discard. Shred the cabbage just before you plan to use it to preserve the vitamin C.

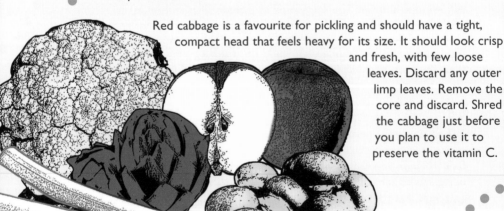

Preparation and cooking

Some vegetables need blanching before pickling, others
need no cooking and some are cooked in the vinegar as part
of the pickling process. The vegetables are immersed in a wet
or dry brine for a specified time, then drained and rinsed thoroughly
under cold running water. The purpose of this is to extract some of the
moisture from the vegetables (which otherwise would dilute the vinegar
and reduce its preserving quality) and keep them firm and crisp and will
also add to the clarity of the pickles. Each vegetable is treated differently
according to type so follow the instructions in individual recipes.

After rinsing, the vegetables are packed into jars so they don't become
squashed or bruised, and then the jars are filled with spiced vinegar almost
to the top. Leave a 12-mm (½ in) space between the vinegar and the top of
the jar. Cold vinegar produces crisp sharp pickles; alternatively the vinegar
can also be heated before pouring into the jars and produces softer pickles.

Sweet pickles are made by simmering the fruits or vegetables with vinegar,
sugar and spices. After potting, the vinegar syrup is boiled down until
reduced, then poured over the fruits into the jars. Shake the jars occasionally during storage to distribute the fruit and syrup evenly. Be careful not to
overcook the fruit in sweet pickles as it should retain a firm texture.

Pickles must be stored in a cool, dark, dry place to prevent discoloura-
tion. They are best left for at least one month before using. Once opened
store in the refrigerator.

What can go wrong?

Soft fruits or vegetables, which have lost their crisp texture, are due to
being stored for too long. Pickles will retain their crisp texture for up
to a year if stored correctly.

Cucumber pickle

This sweet pickle is also known as 'bread and butter' pickle as it is delicious eaten with thickly sliced bread and butter. It is also good with cold meats and cheese.

 3 large cucumbers, thinly sliced

 2 large onions, peeled and thinly sliced

 50 g (2 oz) salt

 600 ml (1 pt) cider or white distilled vinegar

 450 g (1 lb) granulated or caster sugar

 ½ tsp ground turmeric

 1 tsp celery seed

1 tsp mustard seed

1 Arrange the cucumber and onion slices in alternate layers in a large bowl, sprinkling salt between each layer. Cover with a weighted plate and leave to stand for at least 3 hours. Drain off the salty liquid and rinse and dry the vegetables well.

2 Put the cider or vinegar, sugar and spices into a large heavy-based pan, and stir over a low heat, until the sugar has dissolved completely.

3 Add the cucumber and onion and bring to the boil.

4 Boil for 1 minute, then remove from the heat. Remove the vegetables and mustard seeds with a slotted spoon and pack into jars.

5 Boil the vinegar syrup for about 10 minutes until reduced, then remove from the heat and pour over the vegetables to completely cover them.

6 Cover, seal and label when cold.

Makes about 2 kg (4 lb 6 oz)

Mixed pickles

A soft piquant pickle that goes well with cold meat and cheese. You can use courgettes (or zucchini) instead of the marrow if you wish. The turmeric adds a warm, mildly spicy flavour and yellow colour.

Makes
about
1.5–2 kg (4 lb)

 1 medium cucumber

 450 g (1 lb) tomatoes, cut in half and seeds removed

 675 g (1 lb 8 oz) marrow (or yellow squash), peeled and seeds removed

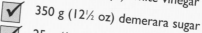 1.1 litres (1¾ pt) white vinegar

 350 g (12½ oz) demerara sugar

25 g (1 oz) salt

15 g (½ oz) ground turmeric

 1 tsp ground mixed spice

 ¼ tsp ground mace

1 Mince or finely chop all the vegetables. A food processor makes short work of this. Put all the ingredients into a large heavy-based pan, stir well and bring to the boil.

2 Reduce the heat and simmer gently for about 2–3 hours until thick and a dark colour.

3 Remove from the heat. Pour into warmed sterilised jars, then cover, seal and label.

Pickled mushrooms

Use small white mushrooms for this recipe. If you wish you can use white wine vinegar instead of white malt vinegar. Mace enhances the flavour of the mushrooms. Leave these pickles for a few days before eating to allow the flavour to develop.

 450 g (1 lb) button mushrooms, stalks removed

 600 ml (1 pt) white malt vinegar

 Whole cloves

10 peppercorns

2 blades of mace

1 Tbsp salt

Makes
about 450 g
(1 lb)

1 Put the mushrooms into a small pan and just cover with water. Add a pinch of salt and bring to the boil. Boil for 10 minutes, then remove from the heat and drain very well.

2 Put the vinegar, spices and salt into a medium heavy-based pan and bring to the boil. Simmer for 10 minutes, then remove from the heat and allow to cool completely. Put the cold mushrooms into jars and pour over the cold vinegar.

3 Cover, seal and label.

Spiced pickled pears

In the days when fruit was only available in season, it was often preserved in this way. These pears are a delicious accompaniment to any cold meats or poultry. You can use apples or quinces instead of pears if you like.

1 Peel, halve (or quarter) and core the pears and put into a bowl of slightly salted water with a dash of lemon juice, to prevent them becoming brown.

2 Mix a little of the vinegar with the spices and put the remaining vinegar and the sugar into a pan with the lemon rind. Heat gently until the sugar has dissolved completely, then add the spice mixture and bring to the boil.

3 Rinse the pears and add to the pan. Simmer gently for about 15–20 minutes, until the pears look clear and are tender but not broken. Remove the pears with a slotted spoon and put into warmed sterilised jars.

- ✓ 1.5 kg (3 lb 5 oz) cooking or hard pears
- ✓ Slightly salted cold water
- ✓ Dash of lemon juice
- ✓ 600 ml (1 pt) white distilled vinegar
- ✓ 1 tsp ground mixed spice
- ✓ ½ tsp grated nutmeg
- ✓ 1 tsp ground cinnamon
- ✓ 450 g (1 lb) granulated or caster sugar
- ✓ Finely pared rind of ½ lemon

4 Discard the lemon peel and boil the liquid in the pan rapidly for about 10–15 minutes, until it has thickened to a syrup.

5 Remove from the heat. Pour over the pears to cover them completely and seal the jars immediately.

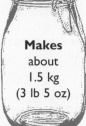

Makes
about
1.5 kg
(3 lb 5 oz)

Spiced pickled blackberries

*Here whole blackberries are covered in a lightly
spiced vinegar syrup and make a tasty and unusual
accompaniment to cold meats, game and cheese.*

Makes
about 1.5 kg
(3 lb 5 oz)

 300 ml (11 fl oz) red wine vinegar

 450 g (1 lb) white or brown sugar

 ½ tsp ground cinnamon

 ½ tsp ground ginger

 ½ tsp ground cloves

1.5 kg (3 lb 5 oz) blackberries

1 Put the vinegar, sugar and spices
into a large heavy-based pan and
heat gently until the sugar has
dissolved. Bring to the boil, reduce
the heat and simmer gently for a
few minutes.

2 Add the blackberries and simmer for about 4–6 minutes,
until the blackberries are soft but still whole. Remove the berries with
a slotted spoon and pack into warmed sterilised jars.

3 Boil the vinegar and sugar rapidly for about
5 minutes, or until the mixture forms a
thick syrup. Remove from the heat, then
pour the hot syrup into the jars of fruit
to cover completely.

4 Cover and seal tightly. Leave for at least
three weeks before using.

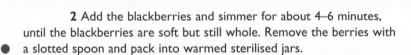

Pickled onions

These crunchy pickled onions are a great favourite and are delicious with cheese, cold meats and poultry, and in salads. If you like sweet pickled onions add the sugar, otherwise omit this. The spices add an aromatic flavour to the onions and vinegar.

1 Put the onions into a large bowl with the salt and mix together. Cover and leave overnight.

2 Rinse thoroughly in cold water and leave to dry on absorbent kitchen paper or on a clean tea towel for about 15 minutes. Pack the onions into cold sterilised jars.

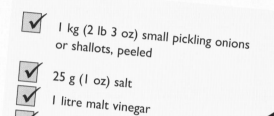

- ✓ 1 kg (2 lb 3 oz) small pickling onions or shallots, peeled
- ✓ 25 g (1 oz) salt
- ✓ 1 litre malt vinegar
- ✓ 1 tsp coriander seeds (optional)
- ✓ 1 tsp peppercorns (optional)
- ✓ 2 Tbsp granulated or caster sugar (optional)

3 Put the vinegar, spices and sugar (if using) into a medium pan and slowly bring to the boil over a low heat, until the sugar has dissolved completely. Cook steadily for 15 minutes, then remove from the heat and allow to cool completely.

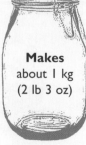

Makes
about 1 kg
(2 lb 3 oz)

4 Strain the vinegar through a sieve over the onions to cover completely. Cover and seal tightly. Store in a cool, dark cupboard for two weeks before eating.

Pickled plums

These piquant plums are delicious with cold pies as well as any cold meats and poultry. You can use small red plums, damsons or greengages in this recipe, and each will give a slightly different result.

 450 g (1 lb) small plums, stalks removed

 300 ml (11 fl oz) white distilled vinegar

 225 g (8 oz) granulated or caster sugar

 Finely pared rind of ½ lemon

 Small piece fresh root ginger, bruised

4 whole cloves, peeled

1 cinnamon stick

1 Prick the plums all over with a darning needle and place in a medium heavy-based pan. Cover with vinegar and add the sugar.

2 Tie the lemon rind and spices in a piece of muslin and add to the pan.

3 Heat gently, stirring, until the sugar has dissolved completely, then bring to the boil. Reduce the heat and simmer very gently, until the fruit is tender, but don't let the skins break.

4 Remove the fruit with a slotted spoon and pack into warmed sterilised jars.

5 Discard the muslin and boil the liquid rapidly for 5 minutes, then remove from the heat. Pour immediately over the plums to cover completely.

6 Cover and seal tightly.

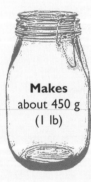

Makes
about 450 g
(1 lb)

Pickled red cabbage

*This is one of the most popular
pickles and is excellent with
cheeses and cold meats.
It is also delicious served as an
accompaniment to meaty stews
and sausages. It is best eaten
within two to three months,
before the cabbage begins to
lose its crispness.*

☑ 2 firm red cabbages, cut into fine shreds across the grain

☑ 110 g (4 oz) salt

☑ 600 ml (1 pt) red wine vinegar

☑ 600 ml (1 pt) distilled malt vinegar

☑ 3 bay leaves

☑ 1 Tbsp juniper berries (optional)

1 Put a layer of cabbage in
a large bowl and sprinkle
with salt. Repeat until all
the cabbage has been used,
ending with a layer of
salt. Leave to stand for
24 hours, then drain
off the liquid.

2 Rinse the cabbage well in
cold water, then drain thoroughly.

3 Heat both vinegars in a large pan and bring to the boil. Reduce the
heat and simmer for 5 minutes, then remove from the heat and
allow to cool completely.

4 Pack the cabbage into cold sterilised jars with the bay
leaves and juniper berries if using. Pour in the cold vinegar
to cover completely.

5 Cover, seal and label. Allow to mature for a week before eating.

Piccalilli

The recipe for 'sweet Indian pickle' was brought to England from the East in the 17th century and became known as piccalilli. Homemade piccalilli is much tastier and has a better texture than the commercial version. It is delicious with cold meats and cheeses. Use a mixture of cauliflower, cucumber, green beans, green tomatoes, pickling onions and marrow.

☑ 1.5 kg (3 lb 5 oz) prepared vegetables (see introduction)

☑ 175 g (6 oz) salt

☑ 2 litres (3½ pt) water

☑ 110 g (4 oz) demerara sugar

☑ 1 tsp ground ginger

☑ 750 ml (1¼ pt) white distilled vinegar

☑ 25 g (1 oz) plain flour

☑ 2 tsp turmeric

☑ 1 Tbsp mustard powder

Makes
about 2 kg
(4 lb 6 oz)

1 Cut all the vegetables into small even-sized pieces and place in a large bowl.

2 Dissolve the salt in the water and pour over the vegetables. Keep the vegetables submerged with a weighted plate and cover the bowl with a cloth.

3 Leave to stand for 24 hours.
Drain the vegetables and rinse thoroughly.

4 Place the vegetables in a large heavy-based pan with
the sugar, ginger and three-quarters of the vinegar, and
bring to the boil.

5 Reduce the heat and simmer gently until as crisp or as
tender as you like them. Crisp vegetables will need only
5 minutes simmering. Remove the vegetables with a
slotted spoon, drain well and put into hot sterilised jars.

6 Mix the flour, turmeric and mustard powder
with the remaining vinegar and stir
into the hot liquid in the pan.
Bring to the boil and boil for
about 1 minute, until thick
enough to coat the back of a
wooden spoon, then remove
from the heat and pour over
the vegetables.

7 Gently bang the jars on a work surface to
remove any air bubbles and top up with more
sauce if necessary.

8 Cover and seal while hot and store for
3 months before using.

Bottling

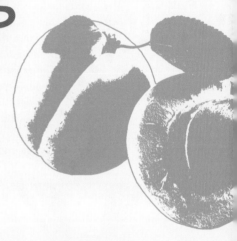

We have Napoleon Bonaparte to thank for the idea of bottling fruit. In 1800 he offered a prize of 12,000 francs to anyone who could create a method of preserving food as a means of providing his armies with daily rations. The winner was Nicolas Appert who put forward his invention of bottling. Bottling fruit has remained steadfastly popular throughout the years and is a marvellous way to preserve a surplus of fruit.

Equipment

Use proper preserving jars with matching lids and close fitting rubber rings and wide necks so the fruits can be packed in easily. These are available from kitchen shops and come in varying sizes so you can bottle large or small quantities. Chipped jars or cracked lids must not be used as the seal will be poor and the contents could be become contaminated.

Kilner (Mason) jars are ideal and are available in a range of sizes. A Kilner jar is a glass jar which has a lid in two sections to ensure an airtight seal. Originally a glass disc sat on top of the jar and was then secured in place with a metal screw band which contains a rubber seal. Nowadays both sections of the lid are usually made from metal. The original Kilner jar is sometimes mistaken for the more widely available glass jar with a rubber seal and a metal hinge, which when closed forms an airtight seal. These jars can be used instead of a Kilner jar.

Jars and lids must be well washed, rinsed well and put into a large pan of cold water. Bring slowly to the boil, then remove from the heat and leave the jars in the water until needed. Don't wipe the jars, just shake off any surplus water.

A sugar or preserving thermometer is advisable, to ensure the correct temperature has been reached.

Ingredients

Fruit must be sound, unbruised, unblemished and just ripe. Rinse the fruit gently under cold running water. Very fragile fruits, such as raspberries, only require a gentle swirl around in a bowl of cold water, then draining on absorbent kitchen paper. Then prepare the fruit as directed in the recipe.

Tomatoes are popular for bottling and there are hundreds of varieties available today – green, orange, yellow, red, tiny, huge, round or plum shaped. Tomatoes hate the cold so are best stored at room temperature. If you do have some in the refrigerator, take them out a few hours before you plan to use them.

Preparation

The fruit is packed into jars as tightly as possible without damaging it. The jars are then filled with cold water or syrup, and then the rubber rings, lids and screw bands are put into place. Give the bands a half turn to loosen them slightly (the glass expands during sterilisation). If using bottling jars with clips instead of screw bands, move the clips slightly to the side of the lids to decrease the pressure to the jars.

Line a deep heavy pan with a thick layer of paper or cloth to prevent the jars cracking. Put the jars in the pan, making sure they don't touch each other and pour in cold water to come right up to the neck of the jars. Cover with a lid or triple thickness of foil.

Very slowly bring the water to simmering point – this should take at least 1½ hours. Follow the directions in individual recipes as some fruits will be required to reach a higher temperature than others. Check by using a preserving thermometer. Do not try to hurry this

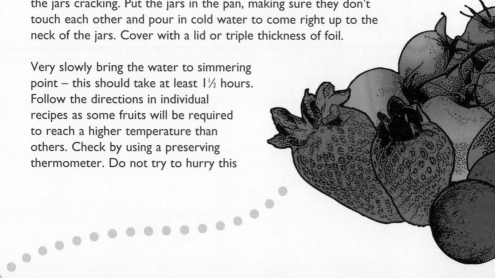

process; if the water is heated too quickly the fruit may rise in the bottles and more time may be needed at the maximum temperature to enable the heat to penetrate the fruit in the centre of the jars.

The temperature must be maintained for 30 minutes. Remove the pan from the heat, then carefully remove the hot jars from the pan. Wear thick oven gloves to do this. Stand the hot jars on a wooden chopping board – not a cold surface or the jars may crack. Tighten the screw bands or move the clips to the centre of the lids and leave to stand for 24 hours.

When cool, remove the screw bands or clips and test that the lids are tightly sealed. If not the fruit is not safe to keep and should be eaten the same day.

Store bottled fruits in a cool, dark, dry cupboard. Check the seals from time to time to ensure the jars are still tightly sealed. Once opened store in the refrigerator.

NB: only fruits and tomatoes should be bottled. Vegetables must not be bottled as the results could prove fatal if the correct temperature is not reached.

What can go wrong?

If the fruit shrinks during storage this is due to air in the jars.
After putting the fruit into the jars, tap the jars to remove any air bubbles.
Mouldy fruits are caused by storing the jars in moist, warm conditions.
Discoloured fruit is caused by storing the jars incorrectly.
Light will bleach their colour.

Bottling individual fruits

Apples: peel, core and slice. They will need 15 minutes at 82°C/180°F.

Apricots: leave whole. They will need 15 minutes at 82°C/180°F.

Blackberries: leave whole. They will need 10 minutes at 74°C/165°F.

Cherries: remove stalks but leave whole. They will need 15 minutes at 82°C/180°F.

Damsons: remove stalks but leave whole. They will need 15 minutes at 82°C/180°F.

Gooseberries: top and tail but leave whole. They will need 15 minutes at 82°C/180°F.

Mulberries: leave whole. They will need 10 minutes at 74°C/165°F.

Peaches: blanch in boiling water for 1 minute and remove the skins. Cut in half and remove stones. They will need 15 minutes at 82°C/180°F.

Pears: use dessert pears only. Cut in half or quarters and scoop out the soft cores. They will need 30 minutes at 88°C/190°F.

Plums: remove stalks but leave whole or cut in half and remove stones. They will need 15 minutes at 82°C/180°F.

Raspberries: leave whole. They will need 10 minutes at 74°C/165°F.

Apples and other hard fruits

Fruits that become brown when exposed to air should be dropped into a bowl of water with a little lemon juice added to prevent this happening.

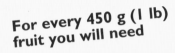

For every 450 g (1 lb) fruit you will need

✓ 150 ml (5 fl oz) syrup (use 225 g/8 oz caster sugar to every 600 ml/1 pt water)

1 To make the syrup, heat the sugar and water in a medium-large pan (depending on the amount of sugar and water used) and slowly bring to the boil for about 2 minutes, until the sugar has dissolved completely. Remove from the heat and allow to cool completely.

2 Pack the fruit (see page 109) into the prepared jars and pour in the cold syrup. This is best done slowly to allow the syrup to seep to the bottom of the jars.

3 Fit on the lids as directed on page 109. Line a deep heavy pan with a thick layer of paper or cloth to prevent the jars cracking. Put the jars in the pan, making sure they don't touch each other and pour in cold water to come right up to the neck of the jars. Cover with a lid or triple thickness of foil.

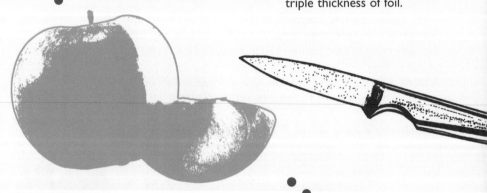

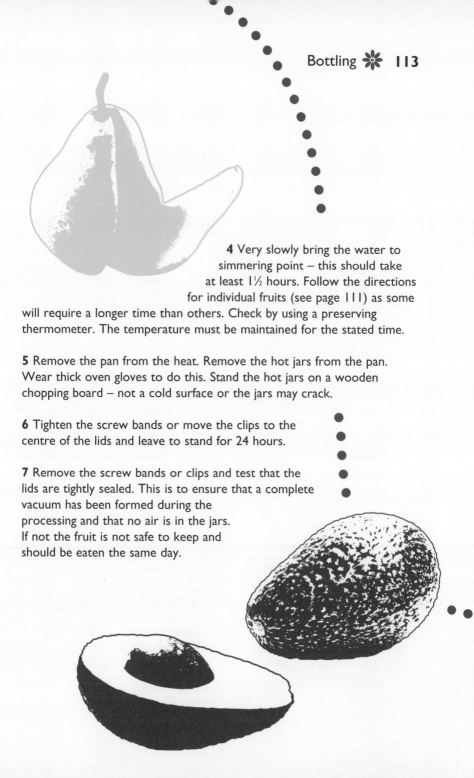

4 Very slowly bring the water to simmering point – this should take at least 1½ hours. Follow the directions for individual fruits (see page 111) as some will require a longer time than others. Check by using a preserving thermometer. The temperature must be maintained for the stated time.

5 Remove the pan from the heat. Remove the hot jars from the pan. Wear thick oven gloves to do this. Stand the hot jars on a wooden chopping board – not a cold surface or the jars may crack.

6 Tighten the screw bands or move the clips to the centre of the lids and leave to stand for 24 hours.

7 Remove the screw bands or clips and test that the lids are tightly sealed. This is to ensure that a complete vacuum has been formed during the processing and that no air is in the jars. If not the fruit is not safe to keep and should be eaten the same day.

Fruit salad

The fruit in this recipe is bottled by a different method. The fruit is packed into hot jars, covered with boiling syrup and placed in a low oven to sterilise the fruit. The success with this method rests in the quick filling and sealing of the bottles as soon as they are removed from the oven.

 450 g (1 lb) caster sugar

 1.1 litres (1¾ pt) water

 1 kg (2 lb 3 oz) Victoria plums, cut in half and stones removed

 225 g (8 oz) seedless grapes

 6 peaches, skinned, cut in half and stones removed

 4 dessert pears, cut in quarters and cores removed

1 Put the sugar and water into a medium pan over a low heat and stir until the sugar has dissolved completely. Bring to the boil and boil for 2 minutes. Preheat the oven to 150°C/300°F (gas 2).

2 Pack an equal quantity of fruit into hot sterilised jars. Pour the boiling syrup over the fruit to within 2.5 cm of the top of the jars. Arrange the jars about 5 cm apart on baking trays lined with newspaper. Cover the jars with lids (but not screw bands) and place in the oven for 1½ hours.

3 Remove from the oven and screw the caps on tightly to seal. Leave to stand for 24 hours.

4 Remove the screw bands or clips and test that the lids are tightly sealed. This is to ensure that a complete vacuum has been formed during the processing and that no air is in the jars, otherwise the fruit is not safe to keep and should be eaten the same day.

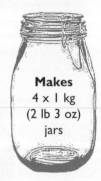

Makes
4 x 1 kg
(2 lb 3 oz)
jars

Bottled tomatoes

1 If using small tomatoes remove the stalks but leave whole. Medium or large tomatoes can be blanched in boiling water to remove the skins, then cut into halves or quarters.

2 Toss the tomatoes in the lemon juice, sugar and salt. Pack tightly into jars, with no air spaces between them.

For every 1.5 kg (3 lb 5 oz) tomatoes you will need

- ✓ 1½ Tbsp lemon juice
- ✓ 1½ tsp salt
- ✓ 1½ tsp sugar

3 Put the jars in a large pan, making sure they don't touch each other and pour in cold water to come right up to the neck of the jars. Cover with a lid or triple thickness of foil. Very slowly bring the water to simmering point – this should take at least 1½ hours.

4 Whole tomatoes will need 30 minutes at 88°C/190°F. Halved or quartered tomatoes will need 40 minutes at the same temperature. Check by using a preserving thermometer. The temperature must be maintained for the stated time.

5 Remove the pan from the heat and carefully remove the hot jars from the pan. Wear thick oven gloves to do this. Stand the hot jars on a wooden chopping board – not a cold surface or the jars may crack. Tighten the screw bands or move the clips to the centre of the lids and leave to stand for 24 hours.

6 Remove the screw bands or clips and test that the lids are tightly sealed. If they are not, the tomatoes are not safe to keep and should be eaten the same day.

Salting

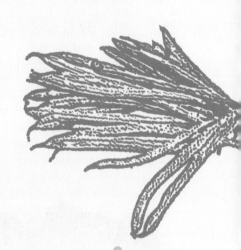

Salting green beans and white cabbage is a time-honoured way of preserving summer and autumn vegetables to use during the winter months. Salt is an excellent preservative and salted vegetables will keep for about six months.

Equipment

Large stone or glass jars are necessary to layer the vegetables with the salt. These must be scrupulously clean and dry.

Ingredients

Vegetables used for salting must be fresh, young and tender, unblemished and completely dry.

Salt has two effects: it draws water from the vegetables by the process of osmosis. Then the salt in the resultant brine sets off the fermentation process of the lactic bacteria. The ensuing fermentation is bacteriologically complex and produces a diverse range of multifaceted flavours. In Europe the most common salted vegetable is white cabbage, which when salted and fermented, is known as sauerkraut.

Salt inhibits attack by harmful micro-organisms. Sea salt or special pickling salt are the best types to use as they are free from impurities and come in the form of crystals. Table salt is mass produced and refined and has been treated to ensure it pours easily.

Spices such as juniper berries and caraway seeds are often used to flavour sauerkraut. Caraway has a warm, pungent aroma and sweet tangy flavour. Juniper berries add a slightly resinous note of pine to the flavour.

Preparation

The vegetables are prepared according to type (runner beans and French beans are the most usual) and will be indicated in the recipes. Use only fresh, young tender beans; wash them and dry thoroughly. The vegetables are then packed well down into the jars, alternately with layers of salt sprinkled generously over them. Begin and end with a thick layer of salt and press down the vegetables as you layer them. Most bacteria cannot survive in a highly salty environment and this is how the food is preserved.

Cover and leave in a cool, dark place for four days. The vegetables will have shrunk, so it is necessary to top up the jars with more vegetables and salt, finishing with a layer of salt. As the salt draws liquid from the vegetables it will form a strong brine. The brine should be kept intact otherwise air pockets will form and the vegetables will deteriorate rapidly and bacteria and mould will develop.

The jars are sealed tightly and stored in a cupboard for up to six months. Don't place the jars on stone or brick as moisture will be drawn out of them.

Before eating the vegetables it is essential to rinse them thoroughly in cold water and then soak them in warm water for two hours. Cook for about 20–30 minutes or until tender. Drain and serve as for fresh vegetables.

What can go wrong?

There's not really anything that can go wrong when salting vegetables. Just remember to rinse them very well before eating or they will be overpoweringly salty.

Runner beans

Runner beans are also known as scarlet runner beans due to their attractive, vivid red flowers, originally the reason they were grown in gardens. Fresh young runner beans are one of the best summer vegetables, succulently tender and packed with flavour. Tiny young beans are very tender and don't need topping, tailing or stringing.

 1.5 kg (3 lb 5 oz) fresh young runner beans, topped and tailed

 450 g (1 lb) coarse or sea salt, not table salt

1 Remove any strings from the sides of the beans if necessary and cut the beans into thin diagonal slices.

2 Put a thick layer of salt in the base of large glass jars or earthenware crock. Add a layer of beans. Repeat until all the beans have been used, ending in a layer of salt. Press each layer of beans down well as you layer them. When the jar is full cover with a lid.

3 Leave in a cool dark place for 4 days, by which time the beans will have shrunk. Top up the jars with more beans and salt, finishing with a layer of salt.

4 Seal tightly and store for up to 6 months.

To serve: rinse thoroughly and cook in simmering water for about 10 minutes, or until tender.

French beans

French or string beans are smaller and rounder than runner beans and have a mild but very pleasant flavour. They originated in Central and South America and were introduced into Europe in the 16th century.

1 Follow the recipe and method as with runner beans (see opposite) but leave the beans whole.

To serve: rinse thoroughly and cook in simmering water for about 10 minutes, or until tender.

French beans
are smaller
and rounder
than runner
beans and have
a mild flavour.

Sauerkraut

The cabbage ferments as it is stored and has a unique and distinctive sour flavour. Homemade sauerkraut is much tastier than the commercial variety and is well worth the time and effort it takes to make. Caraway, bay leaves and juniper berries add an aromatic flavour, but you can omit these if you wish. It is worth making a large amount as it is a lengthy process.

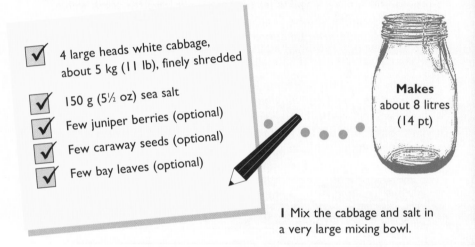

☑ 4 large heads white cabbage, about 5 kg (11 lb), finely shredded

☑ 150 g (5½ oz) sea salt

☑ Few juniper berries (optional)

☑ Few caraway seeds (optional)

☑ Few bay leaves (optional)

Makes about 8 litres (14 pt)

1 Mix the cabbage and salt in a very large mixing bowl.

2 Pack tightly into a clean wooden tub or 9-litre stoneware jar, adding a few juniper berries, caraway seeds and bay leaves, if using.

3 Cover the top of the cabbage with a clean cloth or double thickness of muslin. Add a stopper which fits inside the container or put a plate on top which fits inside the jar or tub.

4 Stand a heavy weight (a stone or brick is ideal) on the plate and leave in a warm room (21°C/70°F) for 4–5 days. When froth appears remove the weight and plate and skim it off. Leave to stand for another 2 days and skim off the froth again. Repeat this process for 2 weeks.

5 The sauerkraut is now ready to eat and can be kept in the refrigerator for several weeks or frozen.

For long-term storage: drain off the brine into a large pan and add the cabbage. Heat to simmering point and immediately put into warmed preserving jars.

Line a deep heavy-based pan with a thick layer of paper or cloth to prevent the jars cracking. Put the jars in the pan, making sure they don't touch each other and pour in cold water to come right up to the neck of the jars. Cover with a lid or triple thickness of foil. Very slowly bring the water to simmering point and simmer for 30 minutes.

Carefully remove the jars from the pan. Wear thick oven gloves to do this. Stand the hot jars on a wooden chopping board – not a cold surface or the jars may crack. Tighten the screw bands or move the clips to the centre of the lids and leave to stand for 24 hours. Remove the screw bands or clips and test that the lids are tightly sealed.

Store the jars in a cool, dark place for up to a year.

To serve: rinse the salty juices out before using. Taste a little and if it is still too salty soak it for about 20 minutes in tepid water, then rinse again. Drain and squeeze out the liquid. Sauerkraut can be eaten as it is or cooked by simmering in a pan of boiling water for about 15–30 minutes until done to your liking. You can also cook sauerkraut by stewing it very slowly for about 2 hours in a pan with just enough water to cover. Alternatively, fry sauerkraut briefly in a little oil in a frying pan, then cover with boiling water and cook until done to your liking.

AUTUMN
Vegetables and herbs
Artichokes (globe and Jerusalem)
Beans (kidney and runner)
Broccoli
Cabbage
Carrots
Celery
Courgettes
Cucumbers
Leeks
Lettuce
Marrows
Mint
Mushrooms
Parsley
Parsnips
Potatoes
Pumpkin
Radishes
Shallots
Spinach
Squash
Swedes
Sweetcorn
Tomatoes
Turnips
Watercress
Zucchini

Fruits
Apples, including crab apples
Blackberries
Damsons
Elderberries
Pears
Plums
Raspberries

WINTER
Vegetables and herbs
Artichokes (globe and Jerusalem)
Beetroot
Brussels sprouts
Cabbage
Carrots
Cauliflowers
Celeriac
Celery
Chicory
Kale
Leeks
Mushrooms
Onions
Parsnips
Potatoes
Rutabaga
Shallots
Swedes
Turnips
Watercress

Fruits
Apples
Pears
Quinces

SPRING

Vegetables and herbs
Artichokes (globe and Jerusalem)
Asparagus
Beetroot
Broccoli
Carrots
Cauliflowers
Celery
Cucumbers
Lettuce
Mint
Mushrooms
New potatoes
Parsley
Rutabaga
Spinach
Spring green cabbage
Spring onions
Swedes
Watercress

Fruits
Apples
Rhubarb

SUMMER

Vegetables and herbs
Artichokes (globe and Jerusalem)
Basil
Beans (broad, kidney and runner)
Cabbage
Carrots
Cauliflowers
Celery
Courgettes
Cucumbers
Lettuce
Marrows
Mint
Mushrooms
Parsley
Peas
Radishes
Spinach
Tomatoes
Watercress
Zucchini

Fruits
Blackcurrants
Cherries
Damsons
Gooseberries
Greengages
Mulberries
Pears
Plums
Raspberries
Redcurrants
Strawberries

UK
Freeman & Harding Ltd
Unit 18, Bilton Road
Erith
Kent DA8 2AN
www.freemanharding.co.uk
(for all sizes and types of preserving jars, lids, covers, preserving pans, thermometers, etc.)

Head Cook and Bottlewasher
8 Church Street
North Walsham
Norfolk NR28 9DA
www.headcook.co.uk
Email sales@headcook.co.uk
Fax 01692 407855
(for stoneware crocks, preserving jars, glass bottles, muslin, etc.)

Just Preserving
Unit 15 Mahoney Green
Rackheath
Norwich NR13 6JY
www.justpreserving.co.uk
(for all sizes and types of preserving jars, lids, covers, preserving pans, thermometers, etc.)

Lakeland
Alexandra Buildings
Windermere
Cumbria LA23 1BQ
www.lakeland.co.uk
(for all sizes and types of preserving jars, lids, covers, preserving pans, thermometers, etc.)

Wares of Knutsford Ltd
PO Box 321
Knutsford WA16 8YQ
www.waresofknutsford.co.uk
(for all sizes and shapes of jars, lids, preserving pans, etc.)

US
Ball
PO Box 529
Daleville, IN 47334
www.freshpreserving.com
(for all sizes and types of jars, lids, bands, covers, etc.)

To find many useful links to canning and preserving supplies, please visit:
http://housewares.about.com/od/canning preserving/a/canningsupplies.html